SOVIET RUSSIAN DIALECTICAL MATERIALISM

[DIAMAT]

J. M. BOCHEŃSKI

SOVIET
RUSSIAN DIALECTICAL
MATERIALISM

[DIAMAT]

D. REIDEL PUBLISHING COMPANY

DORDRECHT-HOLLAND

Der Sowjet-Russische Dialektische Materialismus (Diamat)
First published by
Francke Verlag, Bern – Switzerland
Translated from the German by Nicolas Sollohub and revised after the third
German edition by Thomas J. Blakeley

1963

Printed in The Netherlands by D. Reidel, Dordrecht

TABLE OF CONTENTS

SYSTEMATIC SECTION

TABLE OF CONTENTS

Ignorance is not an argument

People belonging to no party are hopeless bunglers in philosophy
just as much
as they are bunglers in politics

LENIN

PREFACE TO THE FIRST EDITION

This book offers a critical outline of the sources of the history, of the spirit and of the doctrines of present-day Soviet Russian Dialectical-Materialism ('Diamat'), i.e. of the philosophical foundations of Marxism-Leninism. It is scarcely necessary to stress the usefulness of a short outline of this kind, as Russian sources are not easily accessible in the West and as it is of considerable interest to know the doctrines which make up the faith of the Communists* in all countries.

The material for this book was first made public in a series of lectures at the University of Fribourg (Switzerland), first in French in the summer term of 1949, later in English at the Summer School in the same year. The French text, slightly expanded, was translated into German by Miss M. Hoerkens, Dipl. rer. pol. Various imperfections in the wording of the text and in the bibliography can be explained by the process of formation of this book. The author hopes that such imperfections will not prove disturbing.

PREFACE TO THE SECOND EDITION

Considerable difficulty arose in the preparation of this edition from the fact that since Stalin's 'demotion' as a 'classic' and as an unquestioned authority (February 25, 1956), the situation in Dialectical Materialism in the USSR has become somewhat strange: actually all the literature on Dialectical Materialism ought to be re-written since almost all of it has slavishly followed Stalin's interpretation; at the time of writing, however, (August 1956) this – so far as I know – has not happened; indeed, it is difficult to imagine how this could have been effected so quickly.

On the other hand Stalin's interpretation of Lenin's ideas, though often superficial, seems to be substantially correct; and Lenin remains the unquestioned authority in Soviet Russia and in all the Communist countries. And so if something different is to replace Stalinism in the

* The term 'Communist' is here applied not just to anyone who supports collectivism, but exclusively to the members of a party which accepts Lenin, according to the currently valid interpretation of his doctrine in the USSR.

sphere under discussion, it is most likely that this will find expression merely in a different way of marshalling the material and in small alterations of detail. For these reasons I have decided to do what the dialectical materialists themselves still do, namely to present Dialectical Materialism on the basis of Stalin's interpretation of it and of the literature based on it. The first edition of my book was sold out unexpectedly soon; the new edition had, therefore, to be prepared on short notice. Accordingly I have added references only where some really new material was available. In the process it was observed that such new material was very scarce: for the greater part it expressed itself in the increased emphasis laid on the so-called 'non-antagonistic oppositions'. Admittedly, various changes have taken place in the marginal spheres of logic, psychology, ethics, but these are outside the scope of Dialectical Materialism in the strict interpretation of the word.

The text was revised and corrected in the light of specialist criticism (Prof. H. Kline's excellent criticism was particularly useful). I have also formulated new judgments, which I have developed in the interval, especially in regard to dialectics and to ethics. The historical part was brought up to date to July 1956 and the bibliography augmented.

It is impossible to name all the scholars who have helped me increase my knowledge since the publication of the first edition. But I should like to make two exceptions by expressing my thanks specifically to the above-mentioned Prof. G. L. Kline and to Dr. Peter Sager; I have learnt a great deal from them both. Furthermore I am particularly grateful to Dr. Sager for helping me with bibliographical material and for allowing me to make use of his outstanding library on the subject.

TRANSCRIPTION RULES

In the matter of transcription, we have used a modified Czech alphabet which has the advantage of rendering Russian characters into easily recognizable Latin equivalents with the following exceptions: 'š' = 'sh' as in 'shoe'; 'č' = 'ch' as in 'chew'; 'ž' = 'g' as in 'rouge'; 'x' = 'ch' as in 'loch'. The apostrophe stands for the 'soft' sign (*mjagkij znak*). An exception to these rules has been made for those Russian proper names which have an accepted anglicized form.

ABBREVIATIONS

AD   – Engels: *Anti-Dühring*
BSE   – *Bolšaja Sovetskaja Enciklopedia*
DM   – Stalin: *Über dialektischen und historischen Materialismus* [1]
FT   – Lenin: *Filosofskie tetradi* [2]
KFS   – Judin and Rozental': *Kratkij filosofskij slovar'* 1940, [3] 1954
LAW – Lenin: *Ausgewählte Werke*
LF   – Engels: *Ludwig Feuerbach*
ME   – Lenin: *Materialismus und Empiriokritizismus*
MEM – Lenin: *Marx – Engels – Marxisme*
Pr   – *Proekt Programmy Kursa Dialektičeskogo Materializma* (1948)
VF   – *Voprosy Filosofii*
Žd   – Ždanov, A. A.: *Vystuplenie* (Speech of June 24, 1947) [4]
ZF   – *Zapiski filosofii*

[1] Quoted according to the text of *Geschichte der Kommunistischen Partei* . . . 1947.
[2] All the quotations are taken from the original texts except for those from '*Fragmente über Dialektik*'. This was published in a German translation as part of ME and is quoted as 'FT – ME'.
[3] All references are to the second (1940) edition except where otherwise stated.
[4] Quotations are taken from VF 1947,1.

SOURCES AND METHOD

We have attempted to present a critical study of *Russian* Dialectical Materialism in its essential features as it is taught *at the present time* (1956). It is impossible to understand this Dialectical Materialism correctly by studying it only at second hand in the writings of Western European or American Bolshevists and 'fellow travellers'. For such writers are all too frequently bent on propaganda and seek to adapt Russian Dialectical Materialism as much as possible to the mentality of Westerners. In doing so they take liberties in their interpretation which would be quite unthinkable in Russia. Non-Bolshevists, too, when they try to explain 'Marxism' often follow an interpretation which is diametrically opposed to the Russian one: Desroches' book is a classical example of such a non-Russian interpretation of Marxism, nay of Stalin himself.

This makes it essential to go back to the Russian sources. These sources can be divided into five categories of unequal importance:

1] *The Classics.* Such were until 1956 Marx, Engels, Lenin and Stalin. But Marx's and Engels's works were accepted as 'classics' only in Lenin's interpretation and Lenin in his turn only as interpreted by Stalin. They, therefore had to be used with care. Now that Stalin is declared to have committed many mistakes the situation is obscure. It would be logical to assume that he is no longer accepted as a classic; in the realm of philosophy, however, there is insufficient evidence for such an assumption. At any rate, Lenin remains the basic authoritative classic. As for Mao Tse-tung, there are insufficient grounds for considering him as a classic even though his position has been considerably strengthened by Stalin's 'demotion'.

2] *The Official Decisions* of the Central Committee of the Party, Ždanov's speeches, etc. which are binding, though they have not yet acquired the status of classics. In our opinion Mao Tse-tung's writings belong to this category.

3] *Semi-official Texts.* Here two publications were particularly significant. First, the *Short Philosophic Dictionary* edited by P. Judin and M. Rozental' which, apart from some historical data and a few comments, consists almost exclusively of quotations from Lenin and Stalin. And second, the programme for an advanced course in Dialectical and Historical

Materialism published in 1948 by the Institute of Philosophy of the Academy of Sciences of the USSR. So far these two publications have not been replaced even though they were both composed along lines sanctioned by Stalin. Indeed it is doubtful whether a substitute will be found for them on any essential point.

4] Textbooks by acknowledged *leaders of philosophic thought* (M. B. Mitin, M. A. Leonov, M. M. Rozental', etc.).

5] *Other literature.* Here one must be very careful when using works published before 1931, especially if their authors were condemned as, for instance, was the case with Bukharin and Deborin. Nevertheless, even in such writings can be found material which can contribute to a better understanding of the doctrine.

Out of the study of this literature arises the following picture. Every essential element in present-day Russian Dialectical Materialism is contained in Lenin's works; every such element is accepted in the form and interpretation assigned to it by Stalin in the above-mentioned essay and, to a lesser degree, by Judin and Rozental' in their dictionary. In *no single essential point* has Russian philosophy gone beyond these two works. On the one hand, this was specifically stated by M. P. Baskin at the Congress of Philosophers (1947) even *before* Ždanov's speech on June 19 of that year – none of those present disagreed with this statement, on the contrary, many speakers supported Baskin's opinion. And, on the other hand, G. A. Wetter, who not so long ago undertook some deep-going research into Soviet philosophical literature, was unable to find one single statement of fundamental importance which was not already contained in the above-mentioned dictionary. Nor did G. L. Kline find anything substantially new in the last few years (1956). The author's own investigations fully confirm this. Admittedly in the recent past the *attitude* of Soviet philosophers has changed on more than one point, but the *doctrines* have remained exactly the same, apart from a few deviations in certain marginal spheres of philosophy.

HISTORICAL SECTION

THE WESTERN ORIGINS

I. GENERAL VIEW. Present-day Dialectical Materialism has three different sources: Marxism, Russian revolutionary ideologies and Lenin's thought. Lenin fused the other two into one under the impact of his powerful personality. It is impossible to understand Dialectical Materialism in the USSR without, at the same time, taking these three factors into account. A detailed study of its development will establish the following filiation for Leninism.

Around the middle of the nineteenth century the German intellectuals were influenced by one of two philosophic currents; by Hegel's philosophy or scientific materialism. Feuerbach, a disciple of Hegel, adapted Hegel's doctrine to the materialistic approach; and Marx was directly influenced by Feuerbach. Marx's friend and collaborator, Engels, perfected this philosophy and became the founder of Dialectical Materialism. Lenin's materialism goes back as far as this, even though he has also been much influenced by Russian thought. The following diagram can serve to illustrate the genesis of Lenin's philosophy:

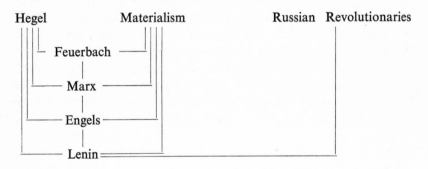

This diagram rather over-simplifies the historical situation (for instance, many a Russian revolutionary thinker was also influenced directly by Marx), but by and large it does illustrate the main relationships.

In this chapter we propose to present briefly the Western sources of Leninism; i.e. the philosophy of Marx and Engels, and their origins as well. This will be followed by a brief exposition of the Russian sources and of Lenin's doctrine itself.

9

2. THE HISTORICAL AND IDEOLOGICAL BACKGROUND. Every phi-losopher who attributes to the body and to the environment some influence on the spirit must acknowledge the validity of the principle of sociologi-cal method. This does not by any means imply that he is of necessity a materialist (i.e. one who is bound to consider the economic factors as the only really decisive ones), but he must nevertheless admit that social conditions and, more particularly, economic conditions play an important part in forming an ideology. Unfortunately, it has been impossible, so far, to draw from this principle deductions which would be fruitful for the history of philosophy. It would seem that the complexity of life and the absence of scientific proof have made it impossible, so far, for the history of philosophy to derive proper benefit from the study of social and economic factors. It is possible to outline the general framework within which history takes its course, but it remains impossible to explain thereby the evolution of the various spiritual tendencies. Even so it is of some value to represent briefly the characteristic features of that period; this does help us understand – at any rate partially – the various phenomena even though we cannot fathom their ultimate origins.

Both Hegel and Comte recognized quite correctly (independently from each other and in sharp contrast to the generally accepted opinion of their contemporaries) that the so-called 'modern' age was, in fact, a form of 'middle ages' between two authentic cultural periods; between, on the one hand, the Christian Middle Ages – characterized by a well-knit culture and social order – and, on the other, an age still to come. Unlike ancient Greece and the Middle Ages our modern age has not created such a social order and culture. To the whole of this period can be applied the well-known epithet, which was originally applied only to the nineteenth century, that it was a 'starry-eyed servant of the Universal Spirit'. For this period is marked by certain features inherited from the past and exaggerated in the process; at the same time it forms a sharp contrast to the past.

Scholasticism, the heritage of the Middle Ages, survives primarily in modern *rationalism*. It was scholasticism which developed and spread the belief in the rational order of the world and in the possibility of recogniz-ing it through rational analysis. This rationalism became wildly exag-gerated in the course of recent centuries. Partly due to the progress of natural sciences, rationalism became a real cult in which reason was deified. Reason was credited with the ability to penetrate everything and to achieve everything. Another feature of modern thought which is of Christian, though not of mediaeval, origin is the belief in *progress*, in perfectibility. This idea was first formulated by St. Augustine; it suffered a setback in the Middle Ages but became powerful again in the eighteenth century for reasons, incidentally, which are quite unknown. In the nineteenth century this belief developed, quite like rationalism, into a veritable cult of progress. It would not be an exaggeration to say that rationalism and belief in evolution are among the principal dogmas of nineteenth century European philosophy.

A third idea which had an almost equally fundamental importance for the nineteenth century arose, unlike the first two, in opposition to mediaeval thought: this was *monism*. This idea turned away from the pluralistic and theistic conception of the world and came eventually to deny the existence of God or to identify him with the universe. In the seventeenth century, Spinoza, with his monism, was a rather isolated phenomenon; but in the nineteenth, the monistic view was accepted by almost all European philosophers. A twofold anti-personalist tendency was reflected in this. For one thing, the universe was conceived as the only *being* and man, to use Spinoza's terminology, as merely a *modus* or manifestation of this *being*; thus robbed of the direct and personal link with God – which he had in the Christian view of the world – man became nothing but a part of nature. From this point of view, modern thought is anti-humanistic in the extreme.

The emergence of one further element associated with this nineteenth century trend can perhaps be more easily explained than that of the others, by reference to the social conditions of the time. The Middle Ages reflected the firm social structure of the time and was an extremely 'social' age. With the Renaissance and the decay of the mediaeval social structure, individual man asserted himself against society, the Reformation and Liberalism being but two examples. This individualism was driven *ad absurdum*; philosophy often made man the centre of the universe. In Kant can be seen the classical representative of this attitude. His revolution, which he himself likened to that of Copernicus is, in spite of all the 'transcendental' elements of his philosophy, a Ptolemaic counter-revolution. This individualistic rebellion petered out at the beginning of the nineteenth century; the constantly increasing interdependence of men, in a world which was being modified gradually by technology, was partly responsible for this. However, it is worth noting that the reaction against individualism manifested itself in the sphere of philosophy much sooner than in other spheres. Indeed, philosophy regained its inner equilibrium through the reintroduction of the social idea. Up to then, philosophy had been rent asunder by mutually contradictory tendencies: on the one hand, it extolled the universe almost to the extent of negating the individual; on the other hand, it was inclined to obey the individualistic tendency and to extol this same individual – to the detriment and disregard of both society and the universe. It is not surprising, therefore, that monism should be establishing its supremacy just at this moment; for it became quite clear that the individual would be stifled. To begin with, this took place only in the philosophers' speculations. The masses, and even the educated people, continued to retain their faith in the anti-social rebellion. The two conceptions rub shoulders awkwardly in the Marxist doctrine.

At any rate, if one takes philosophy in the nineteenth century by itself, one can say that it was rationalistic, monistic and that it believed in evolution. Of course these general features expressed themselves quite differently and were interpreted differently in the various systems of philosophy. Two of these systems, Hegelianism and Scientific Materialism, are of particular interest to us here.

3. HEGEL. After Fichte and Schelling, Georg Wilhelm Friedrich Hegel (1770–1831) is the third of those philosophers who are described as 'German Idealists'; of the early nineteenth century philosophers, he exerted the greatest influence on his contemporaries and, indirectly, on our philosophy. He followed Immanuel Kant (1724–1804) whose idealism he adopted; reality is determined by the notion and the distinction between subject and object has no meaning except in consciousness – a concept which is badly defined in Hegel. There is but one reality (monism), namely, the universal spirit (radical spiritualism), which assumes various forms as it evolves. Reality is understood organically; the whole is greater than the sum of its parts and the parts exist only as contained in the whole and for the sake of the whole (metaphysical totalism). With Hegel, this latter doctrine is founded on an ultra-realism based on the problem of the universals. These universals have, for Hegel, an existence of their own; but they are interpreted in a special way (the universal is called 'concrete').

The spirit which moulds reality evolves into ever more perfect forms (optimistic evolutionism). This evolution is considered to be, at any rate partially, independent of time (logical evolution). It takes place in a dialectical fashion: the thesis is always opposed by an antithesis; both are at the same time retained and dissolved in a synthesis; this synthesis, in its turn, is the thesis for a new antithesis etc., etc. This is not a slow and progressive development, but an evolution in fits and starts which now and again manifests new qualities; for instance, life, consciousness, etc. The higher quality cannot be deduced from the lower (categorial pluralism). The development is strictly determined by the laws of the spirit. There exists neither chance nor free will (determinism). Everything that is real is rational and everything that is rational is at the same time real. There is no room in Hegelianism for the fortuitous, the uncertain or the inexplicable. Hegel professed Christianity and sought to fit religion into his system (as one phase of the evolution of the evolving spirit), but it is self-evident that his monism and his rationalism exclude every supernatural religion and every form of theism. In the sociological sphere, Hegel is a conservative; in his eyes everything that is, including the state that happens to exist at the moment, is necessary and rational.

4. SCIENTIFIC MATERIALISM. Scientific materialism was associated in eighteenth century France with a number of *encyclopédistes* (J. O. LaMettrie, 1709–1751; E. Bonnet, 1720–1793; P. H. D. von Holbach, 1723–1789; D. Diderot, 1713–1784 and Cl. A. Helvetius, 1715–1771). In Germany, towards the middle of the nineteenth century, its evolution was taken further by Jakob Moleschott (1822–1893), Ludwig Büchner (1824–1899) and Karl Vogt (1817–1895). In 1854 it emerged as a powerful force in the famous 'Dispute over materialism' (16 September). It enjoyed powerful support from two intellectual currents; from German Positivism embattled against Hegelianism (Ernst Laas, 1837–1885; Friedrich Jodl, 1848–1914) and, above all, from the supporters of the theory of evolution which spread rapidly after the appearance of Charles Darwin's (1809–1882) *Origin of Species* (1859). There are many points on which these doctrines are not in agreement, but they all contributed to the emergence of a fairly homogeneous philosophy of life. This philosophy became the creed of the majority of German intellectuals in the second half of the nineteenth century and found its most characteristic expression in the

well-known work by Ernst Haeckel (1834–1919), *Die Welträtsel* (1899). (=The Riddle of the Universe).

The following features are characteristic of this philosophy. First and foremost, it is a *realistic* philosophy; reality exists independently of our perceptions and outside of them. It is also *monistic;* there is only one *being (ein Seiendes)* in the world. This monism is *materialistic;* reality is material and mind is a product of matter and a function of it. Furthermore, the conception of reality is *mechanistic;* matter as such is lifeless and is set in motion by extraneous forces. All that exists is conditioned by a time-space relationship and by the local movement of particles of matter. As regards the problem of the universals, this materialism is *nominalistic;* it claims that there are no universals, not even general concepts, but only names of kinds. Organisms are explained in a mechanistic way as being combinations of particles fitted together; the organism is merely the name for such a combination. This doctrine also professes a belief *in evolution;* but the development, a mere matter of chronology, manifests itself in small changes of a purely quantitative nature and adds no new element apart from increasing the multiplicity of atomic combinations. This leads to the conclusion that all qualitatively higher phenomena (life, consciousness, mind, etc.) can be traced back to locally limited movements of matter *(categorial monism)*. In spite of their nominalism, the materialists are radical *determinists*. They are *rationalists* too; for it is their belief that scientific methods can enable man to fathom all of reality. They are impassioned atheists, opponents of all religions of revelation and they hate Christianity. In its place they want to set up an optimistic religion based on science and on belief in the progress of humanity. This doctrine is curiously contradictory to their own system which, after all, does not admit that any human value can exist as an independent concept. For them philosophy is merely the sum of all sciences and has no method of its own.

5. COMPARISON AND CRITICISM OF THE TWO TRENDS. It is evident that these two philosophical doctrines are mutually exclusive, radically and unreconcilably so. Indeed, Hegelianism is a spiritualistic philosophy which allows plenty of space for spiritual values; it is an organic type of philosophy, a pluralistic one, in the categorial sense, and an idealistic one. On the other hand the existence of the spirit is just what scientific mate-

rialism denies, while refusing to recognize any spiritual values. (In Feuerbach's words *'Der Mensch ist, was er ißt'* [1]) – i.e. 'Man is what he eats' – the German pun cannot be rendered in English). Scientific materialism is mechanistic, monistic in the categorial sense, and extremely realistic. Furthermore, the fundamental conception of philosophy is radically different in the two camps.

Nevertheless, numerous points of contact can be found between these two doctrines, however different they may be. Both are rationalistic; both are monistic; both are convinced believers in progressive evolution; both repress the individual; finally both are anti-Christian. Even if Hegel did not himself draw this deduction from his system, it is an evident inconsistency that he did not do so, and his disciples have certainly recognized this. There is also a romantic kernel to be found in both doctrines. For the belief in a dark force which, as it unfolds itself, brings up a better future is indeed an essentially romantic feature. Admittedly such a romantic feature does not fit easily into the framework of materialism, yet it is just this element which has lent it such force. There was a boundless enthusiasm for science, which was expected to create a paradise on earth, and for an evolution which, for some unspecified reason, was expected always to bring forth more and more perfect forms. Both doctrines are to a high degree anti-humanistic; they leave no room for man and condemn the concept of individual personality. Yet the sentiment which inspired the champions of these doctrines was unquestionably romantic and humanitarian.

Looked at in historical perspective, these features, which are common to the two conflicting doctrines, can be easily explained on the basis of the mentality obtaining in the nineteenth century. It is not difficult to judge the two philosophies from the Christian point of view; they contradict Christianity by rejecting revelation and in their 'Promethean' attitude. They can be considered as sins of human pride when they claim the ability to comprehend everything and to achieve everything – e.g. salvation – through human means alone. But a far more complex judgment results if one views Hegelianism and Materialism from the technical point of view of philosophy.

There is no doubt that Hegelianism contains valuable elements; for instance, the energetic (though exaggerated) championing of the spirit, of spiritual values, of evolution – which then represented something novel –

of historical perspective and other elements. But Hegelianism is distorted by two fundamental ideas: idealism and the dialectic. Hegel accepted idealism on Kant's authority without any kind of critical proof. It is an untenable point of departure and has been abandoned by an increasing number of European thinkers. The dialectic, based on a view of the multiplicity of aspects of being and of becoming – in itself correct – has adopted a form which is simply devoid of all sense. It weighed heavily on Engels' philosophy and, through him, on Lenin's. When compared with Hegelianism, Materialism is a rather scanty doctrine; but it has the merit of being a healthy reaction against Hegel's exaggerated idealism and spiritualism. Materialism does not tackle in real earnest any philosophical problem – not even the fundamental one of the nature of matter. To such questions, which it tackles superficially, it frequently offers strikingly primitive answers. At any rate, this form of materialism is nowadays completely untenable in view of the progress of physics; this was clearly recognized by Lenin. It is tragic that Marx and Lenin should be bound to this system of philosophy just for want of a better one.

6. FEUERBACH. After Hegel's death in 1831, his school split up and there arose two groups, among others: one group represented the 'Right' and interpreted the master's doctrine about the rational nature of reality in the conservative sense and retained his religious attitude; another group, on the 'Left', interpreted the same doctrine in a revolutionary sense. For them, only the rational was real; i.e., one must make reality rational by modifying it.

One of the Left Wing Hegelians, Ludwig Feuerbach (1804–1872), exerted a very great influence on Marx. The elements of his doctrine which were of prime importance to the formation of Marxism are as follows:

First of all, Feuerbach, while retaining Hegel's dialectic, carried out a 'materialistic inversion' of Hegelianism. In his eyes, the reality which develops is not spirit, but matter. Thus he fused Hegelianism with scientific materialism and created the foundations for the Dialectical Materialism which arose from this fusion.

Secondly, he attacked religion. In his famous book *Das Wesen des Christentums* (1841) he subjected religion to a critical analysis, based on psychology, which, he thought, proved that God was nothing but man himself and a creation of man.[2]

In the place of Christian theism he set up a religion of *man*. When he said, 'the human is divine' or '*homo homini Deus est*', there was, in this assertion, a certain element of radical humanism which often manifested itself in curiously 'existentialist' expressions.

Finally, Feuerbach emphasized the supreme importance of practical experience as the basis of knowledge; thus his conception of knowledge is realistic. Feuerbach was not a scientific materialist; he was not a mechanist or a categorial monist. He recognized that philosophy has its own method, namely the dialectic.

7. MARX. Karl Marx (1818–1883), the founder of 'scientific' socialism, was first and foremost a sociologist and an economist. As a philosopher, he stemmed from the Hegelian Left. He was influenced particularly by Feuerbach; from him he took such fundamental ideas as his materialism linked with dialectic, his humanism and his atheism. In Marx can be found most of the doctrines which were later taken over by Lenin which we shall describe in the sequel. Not all elements of Marx's doctrine are equally important; his originality is based, above all, on the following three points:

First of all Marx is the founder of *Historical Materialism* which claims that it is the economic factors which ultimately determine the content of social consciousness (science, art, religion, politics, etc.). This consciousness is only a reflection, the 'superstructure', of economic conditions.

Secondly, Marx developed the *theory of the inevitability of the progress of society*, which cannot but lead, through the class struggle, to *Communism*. Communism will free man from enslavement. In spite of the determinism which he usually displayed, Marx believed that it was the task and mission of the proletariat to bring about this liberation; the proletariat had the messianic vocation of bringing about Communism through revolution.

Finally – and this is one of the most striking traits of his philosophy – he preaches the twofold *significance of the practical*. On the one hand, only practical experience can lead to a correct understanding free from errors and distortions. On the other hand, it is no longer the task of philosophy merely to interpret the world, but to modify it.[3] The element that made materialism 'dialectical' is not worked out in really great detail by Marx.

His most important philosophical works are the following: *Die Heilige Familie, oder Kritik der 'Kritischen Kritik', gegen Bruno Bauer und Konsorten* (1845 in collaboration with Engels); *Die deutsche Ideologie* (1846, published for the first time in Russian in 1932 and in 1933 in German by Rjazanov); *Elend der Philosophie, eine Antwort auf Proudhons Philosophie des Elends* (1847). Equal importance is attached to his economic masterpiece *Das Kapital* (Volume I in 1887; volumes II and III were edited by Engels, volume IV by Kautsky).

8. ENGELS. Friedrich Engels (1820–1895) was from 1844 on Marx's closest friend and collaborator; so much so, indeed, that it is often difficult to distinguish their respective contributions to the common doctrine (they published several works in collaboration, including the famous *Communist Manifesto* of 1848). In Russia today it is held by all writers that the doctrine of the two is indivisible. But this goes rather too far.* Admittedly Engels shared his friend's fundamental conceptions; but he stressed certain points in Marx's doctrine to such an extent that he thereby gave a distinctive tendency to Marxism which is rejected by some twentieth century Marxists. These points are particularly important in his doctrine:

He gave Marxism a more speculative, a *metaphysical* direction. Marx was concerned above all with Historical Materialism as a basis for his theory of economics and his revolutionary doctrine. Engels laid the metaphysical and methodological foundations of this materialism which transcended the historical framework and encompassed the whole of nature.

This was achieved by his laying greater stress on the *dialectical* factor. Hegel's dialectic, turned upside down, was in great measure extended by Engels and applied to all the individual spheres of philosophy.

---

* In support of the absolute identity of views between Engels and Marx reference is often made to a remark in Chapter 4 of the book *Ludwig Feuerbach*. It is therefore useful to quote its most significant part: "I cannot myself deny the fact that before and during my forty years of collaboration with Marx I had a certain independent share in establishing and developing the theory. But the major part of the leading fundamental ideas, especially in the *fields of economics and history*, and above all their definitive, exact formulation is Marx's contribution. What I did contribute, except in a few specialized fields, was something which Marx *was quite capable* of achieving without me." (LF 49 et seq.) (Author's italics). First of all it is quite clear that Engels is speaking here of economic and historical but not of philosophical doctrines, and secondly, that he does not deny having developed the latter himself. It is Engels who is the founder of *Dialectical* Materialism.

Finally, he appears to have been much more strongly influenced by *scientific materialism* than Marx was. No wonder, therefore, that Communist writers, with Lenin at their head, turn to Engels rather than to Marx for their most important quotations on Dialectical Materialism. Indeed, Engels forms the bridge between Marx and Lenin.

His principal philosophical works are: *Ludwig Feuerbach und der Ausgang der klassischen deutschen Philosophie* (1886); *Herrn Dührings Umwälzung der Wissenschaften* (in collaboration with Marx, 1877–1878; invariably called 'Anti-Dühring' by the Communists); and *Dialektik der Natur* (1873–1883; published for the first time by Rjazanov in 1925).

9. OBSERVATIONS ON MARXISM. Marx's long personal evolution and the great multiplicity of elements contained in his doctrine have resulted in different interpretations of his theory; so different indeed that today there exists quite a number of mutually contradictory forms of Marxism. They all agree in emphasizing the importance of the social factor in human life; also in accepting a certain pragmatism which expresses itself in the conviction that theory must be justified by practice and that, when all is said and done, practice alone is important. But the interpretations of the individual doctrines differ very much. Here we are not interested in the non-Leninist forms of Marxism; as already stated they have, in our opinion, little practical significance. We shall also ignore here the fact that Marxism has played an important rôle in political and moral life. What is important is to identify the fundamental character of Marxist philosophy as opposed to the other currents of thought valid today.

This philosophy synthesizes the main elements of nineteenth century philosophy. It represents an overall logical conclusion drawn from the whole body of modern thought around 1850. That is why it bears within itself the substantial contradictions which form part and parcel of this thought. Indeed, this thought vacillates between extolling the individual and his suppression in favour of the cosmos, between an extreme spiritualism and an equally radical materialism. Seen from this angle, Marxism is today an indubitably reactionary doctrine. Some new tendencies took shape at the beginning of the twentieth century and so the vast period stretching from the end of the Middle Ages to about 1900 might be considered concluded. Marxism – especially in the form given it by Engels – is the final and most radical expression of an epoch which has disappeared forever.

On the other hand this Marxism does contain at least two positive elements which are likely to be pursued further by present-day thinkers. These are: (1) the emphasis laid on the importance of the social and historical factors and, paradoxically, (2) its fundamental tendency to provide a synthesis for reconciling materialism and extreme spiritualism. Although Marx exaggerated the importance of the economic factor – and thereby restricted the sphere of the social and historical viewpoints – and his crude materialism interfered with the emergence of a synthesis, nevertheless these two fundamental ways of viewing things constitute, in themselves, an undoubtedly positive and viable element in the philosophy of the founder of socialism. But present-day Dialectical Materialism must not be identified too closely with this Marxism because it contains extraneous elements which we shall now attempt to describe.

REFERENCES: [1] Feuerbach, *Nachlaß,* II, 73. [2] Feuerbach, *Werke,* VI, 361. [3] LF 76 (eleventh thesis on Feuerbach).

II. THE RUSSIAN ORIGINS: LENIN

1. OBSERVATIONS ON METHOD. What was said in the preceding chapter about the sociological and economic method, applies fully to the Russian sources of Dialectical Materialism. Let it be noted that in such an investigation one often meets with nonsensical explanations of relationships. It is, for instance, clearly absurd to speak of the 'Asiatic' character of Communism. There is neither a uniform 'Asiatic' character nor an 'Asiatic' culture; many very different cultures exist in Asia. Any attempt to stress the 'Slavic' character must overlook the important fact that the Slavic peoples are divided, by their cultures, into two extremely different groups: the Western and the Eastern Slavs. So significant is this division that the only link between the two groups is the considerable resemblance between their languages. It is equally absurd to speak of a Russian 'race', for there is no such thing. Modern nations are identifiable, not because they belong to a certain race, but because they have a certain culture which is conditioned by history. Whoever wants to obtain a clear picture of the phenomena under discussion must refrain from such simplifications.

Nevertheless, it is true to say that the Russian mentality exhibits features which are remarkably different from those displayed by the mentality of Western European nations. Of course, it would be nonsensical to explain, by reference to this mentality, the entire body of Russian theories which influenced Lenin. But it does play a certain rôle, and we want to assign to it a proper value; this can be done by trying to characterize this mode of thinking which seems so strange to Western Europe. That is why we shall consider first of all the historical and social factors, which distinguish Russia from the rest of Europe, without pretending to provide in the process a complete explanation of the phenomena we see today.

2. HISTORICAL AND SOCIAL BACKGROUND. Let us recollect the following facts from Russian history: Russia received Christianity from Byzantium; in its Western area (Kiev) * there developed a high form of culture which represented a link between the 'Latin' world and Eastern Christianity. In the middle of the thirteenth century this culture was destroyed by nomadic tribes from Central Asia. They held sway over Russia for two centuries and imposed their own culture on her. After the liberation of Moscow, instead of the Kiev tradition being resumed, the Tartar tradition was maintained. The 'Europeanization' of Russia by Peter the Great in the eighteenth century was carried out in a rather despotic-tartar fashion and, in addition, remained superficial.

These historical events have had striking results. From the end of the thirteenth century onwards there was in Russia neither feudalism nor self-government – in the Western sense. In fact, there was not even an organic, graduated structure of society as there was in Western Europe. Furthermore, there was no independent church, no independent aristocracy and no free middle class such as existed in the West. This gigantic country, in which all were subjected to *one single* authority, represented a *corpus politicum* as interpreted by Hobbes, i.e. a conglomeration of human atoms united under the leadership of a central power. Byzantinism in religion prevented struggles between state and church – for all the power was vested in the state, and the church was merely a subordinate organ. So different was the course of history in Russia that this country found it

* Nowadays the population of the Ukraine forms a separate nation which ought to be recognized as being quite distinct from the Russians; but in the thirteenth century this distinction did not exist.

difficult to assimilate Western institutions; this, and propaganda by the Orthodox Church, aggravated what distrust and contempt Russia already had for the West.

Early in the nineteenth century there was no middle class and no free aristocracy in Russia. The social structure consisted of two great classes: the peasants and the bureaucracy. Both were alike in being subjected to the despotic power of the czar. Admittedly there existed the rudimentary beginnings of other classes – among them the working class –, but they were insignificant when compared with the above-mentioned. In the bureaucracy there originated a peculiar social layer, the 'intelligentsia'. This was a fairly important group within society and strove for social reform; but it lacked all possibilities for action and consequently restricted itself to ideological activities – while becoming all the more radical in its views. This intelligentsia played a decisive rôle in the formation of Leninism and will therefore have to be considered again presently.

3. THE RUSSIAN 'SOUL'. A knowledge of this historical evolution and the resulting social structure can help us to understand this spiritual attitude; but we must also take into account certain features which good judges consider particularly characteristic of the Russian mentality. For instance, it is a peculiar Russian trait to take a large scale view of all matters – especially social problems – and to neglect the concrete details of life. The subordination of the Russian Church to the state did not allow a clean separation – as was the case in the West – to occur in Russia between the religious and the secular spheres. Indeed, it fostered the merging of the two. The result was that all social activities acquired a certain hallowed air, an air of sacramental majesty. This is strongly developed in Russian revolutionary thought. Because the individual was unhappily conscious of being enslaved and ground into insignificance by the gigantic machinery of the state, Russian thinkers were driven, almost inevitably, to concern themselves with social problems. Hence the paradox of the Russian mentality; it did not – and could not – work out a clear conception of the dignity of man as the West had done, but displayed a far finer perception of social and human problems. Unable to solve them in practice, on the basis of smaller communities, the Russian views, from a basis of fundamental principles, all these questions in a very abstract manner. He neglects, in the process, facts for the sake of theories. In this,

the Russians are the exact opposite of the empirical English who, not using theory as their starting point, seek to solve all problems on the basis of concrete reality and of experience gained in their immediate surroundings.

All these factors must be taken into account if one wants even to begin to understand Russian 'Messianism'. The existence of the chasm between the Christian ideals, which are deeply rooted in Russian thought, and the deplorable reality around them, deeply affected this people whose thought had anyway been forced by fate to turn towards the general and the abstract. It engendered an apocalyptic vision of a fundamental upheaval which the nation had to carry out in order to free itself from the oppressive conditions of life. This nation which could not comprehend the intellectual world of Western Europe – whose culture was so different from its own – was deeply shaken by many ideas from the West. Sooner or later the idea was bound to arise that Russia alone had preserved the truth and that it alone had the power to liberate and save itself and, eventually, the whole world; not contemporary Russia, but 'true', 'real' Russia, the Russia of the dreamers and theorists. Some responsibility for the intensification of this Messianism lies with the Orthodox Church which, conscious of its mission, ceaselessly preached to the people that the 'Latins' were thoroughly decadent and evil.

4. THE INTELLIGENTSIA. Russian writers characterize the mentality of the Russian intelligentsia of the second half of the nineteenth century and of the early twentieth century as follows. One of its essential features is coextensive with the Russian notion of *principialnost'*; this embraces that special love of the abstract and that interest in great principles which also goes hand in hand with a deep distrust of the concrete. One Russian revolutionary puts it in this way: "I have not been able to find anything that interests me either in men or in women, and so I dedicate myself to the service of mankind".

A mental attitude of this kind is almost always allied to an extreme form of *dogmatism* which lacks the critical and sceptical spirit characteristic of the West.

A profound *dissatisfaction with the prevailing social conditions* forms the basis of a longing for a decisive upheaval. At the same time, almost all the institutions of the modern Western world are lacking in Russia; nor has

Russia experienced the development of capitalism. Therefore, the Russian revolutionary tendencies have quite a different meaning from those in the West. The attitude of the Russian intelligentsia towards the West is one of hatred further intensified by a particular kind of distrust. When Communists are heard referring, with profound contempt, to the 'bourgeoisie', all these factors must be taken into account; for this attitude towards the bourgeois is not only the result of Marx's teaching, but also a typical expression of the mentality of the Russian intelligentsia.

Finally, the members of this class frequently display an *aversion to spiritual values* which could scarcely be found in Western Europe in the same intensity. All this is enshrouded in a deeply religious and Messianic atmosphere. We shall give, as a useful illustration of this, the following short extract from Berdyaev who, as a Russian and a member of this intelligentsia, analysed the mentality of his class in his characteristic and peculiarly searching manner:

"The Russians have displayed a quite peculiar disposition to take up and transform Western ideas. What in the West was a scientific theory which could be criticized as a hypothesis or as relative or partial truth with no pretence to universal validity, *that* was put forward by the Russian intelligentsia as an ultimately valid affirmation bordering on religious revelation. The Russian always seeks for the absolute. It is almost contrary to his nature to display a reserved attitude or to show scepticism in his criticism . . . The Russian intelligentsia considered science as something ultimate, almost divine; hence its methods. In science it believed in Darwinism, but its Darwinism was not only a biological theory which could be discussed, but a dogma; and from that moment all those who rejected this dogma, for instance the supporters of Lamarck, became the objects of its contempt . . . Solov'ev was in fact able to say that the faith of the Russian intelligentsia was founded on the following peculiar syllogism: Man is descended from the monkey, therefore we must all love one another." [1]

5. RUSSIAN REVOLUTIONARY DOCTRINES. As early as the beginning of the nineteenth century the Russian intelligentsia, as described above, rebelled against the prevailing conditions. Poverty, serfdom, corporal punishment, cruel military service lasting twenty-five years and forced marriages were conditions which the members of the Russian intelligentsia

wanted to eradicate. But they had no contact with the people; this and strict supervision by the government made action impossible for them and drove them into elaborating theories.

Towards the middle of the nineteenth century two great spiritual movements can be distinguished: on the one hand, the *Westernizers,* who saw salvation for Russia in the acceptance of Western ideas; the dignity of the individual was all-important to them and they condemned the prevailing forms of Russian life. On the other hand, the *Slavophiles* believed the germs of salvation – not only for Russia herself, but for the entire world – were to be found in the Russian people and in the Orthodox Church.

However, too much importance should not be given to this opposition. Many Westernizers were disappointed in the bourgeois West and thought that Europe would be saved by a refashioned Russia; meanwhile, the Slavophiles were equally opposed to the prevailing forms of the structure of society which, in their opinion, stemmed from the West. Both movements were revolutionary in the extreme and both displayed a typically Russian character in their doctrinaire and semi-religious totalitarianism. Two new movements emerged later on: the nihilists and the populists. The *nihilists* were represented by N. G. Černyševskij (1828–1889), – Marx learnt Russian just to be able to read him – N. Dobroljubov (1836–1861) and, above all, D.I. Pisarev (1841–1868). They were utilitarian materialists of a primitive and crude type. Many of them, sons of Orthodox priests, were distinguished by their outstanding spirit of sacrifice. They preached, with a truly religious zeal, the rejection of all spiritual values. Their influence was particularly noticeable in Russia between 1860 and 1870.

The *populists (narodniki)* were represented by A. I. Željabov (1851–1881), the well-known anarchist P. A. Kropotkin (1842–1921), S. G. Nečaev (1847–1882), P. Tkačev (1844–1885) and M. Bakunin (1814–1876) – another famous anarchist. They were agrarian socialists who saw in the communism of the Russian village the natural foundation for a new order. They wanted to 'go to the people'; a road which the people did not understand and which often led to denunciation to the police. Many of these revolutionary extremists developed an ascetic and, at the same time, Machiavellian morality which Lenin was to adopt. Tkačev in particular seemed to be his direct precursor in this respect. Their influence made itself felt particularly strongly between 1870 and 1880; their periodical *Zemlja i Volja* (Land and Freedom) appeared from 1876 to 1879.

25

Particularly deserving of attention is M. Bakunin who was first a follower and then an opponent of Marx. He was an anti-individualistic anarchist who was remarkable for his intense hatred of God: "If God exists," says Bakunin, "then man is a slave." God was the main supporting pillar of the state which Bakunin wanted to abolish. Tkačev was also important; he formulated two theses which Lenin adopted: one was a radical ethical utilitarianism, similar to, but more radical than that of many other revolutionaries, and the other – in contrast to Bakunin – a theory according to which the state was necessary for revolution. A strong state would exercise the dictatorship which was required for the destruction of the opponents of the revolution. As regards utilitarianism Lenin was also influenced by Černyševskij.

6. RUSSIAN MARXISM. In view of all this it is not surprising that the Russian revolutionaries felt much attracted by Marxism; this doctrine suited their doctrinaire, revolutionary, atheistic and messianic character; for this reason there were many Russians among the early disciples of Marx. His doctrine was taught and discussed in Russia from 1870 onwards, first by N. Ziber (1844–1888), then by many professors of economics. But the real founder of Russian Marxism was Georgi Valentinovič Plekhanov (1856–1918) who, because of his revolutionary activities, was obliged to emigrate and settled in Geneva in 1880. There he founded the first Russian Marxist group, the association for the 'liberation of labour'. The works which he published there are among the best in Marxist literature.

The first socialistic society was founded in St. Petersburg in 1885. Ten years later, in 1895, some twenty similar organizations in that town formed the 'Union for the Struggle and Emancipation of the Working-Class' The first party congress was held in Minsk in 1898 – the second in 1903 – first in Brussels, then in London. In London a discussion about the character of the party arose. Lenin, already a leader in the party, demanded a strict organization while a group led by Z. J. Martov (1873–1923) opposed his views. Lenin had the majority *(bolšinstvo)* for him; his supporters consequently came to be known as *'Bolsheviki'* while the minority *(menšinstvo)* came to be called *'Mensheviki'*. Plekhanov sided with the Mensheviks. An important congress took place in Prague in 1912. In the course of this congress the 'liquidators' were excluded from

THE RUSSIAN ORIGINS: LENIN

the party because they wanted to liquidate the revolutionary movement in favour of action by legitimate means. When the Bolshevik party came to power in the 1917 Revolution, the Mensheviks disappeared or went over to the victors.

During this period Marxist doctrine was engaged in constant battle, first against the populists, then against various Marxist 'deviationists'. Among the latter the following deserve special notice: (a) the 'criticists' (P. Struve, N. Berdyaev, S. Bulgakov), who became 'legal Marxists' and some of whom went over to Christianity; (b) the 'economists' (E. D. Kuskova, Prokopovič), who taught a social form of determinism wherein the workers should restrict themselves to action in the economic field as the revolution was bound to come on its own; (c) the 'empirio-criticists' (A. Bogdanov) and the 'builders of God' *(bogostroiteli)* (A. V. Lunačarskij, M. Gorky, etc.), who were influenced by various philosophic currents in Europe; and finally, (d) the Mensheviks.

In the struggle against these various 'heresies' Lenin, since 1902 the undisputed leader of the party and its outstanding personality, developed that form of Marxism which today is known under the name of 'Communism' and which, as a philosophy, is called 'Dialectical Materialism' ('Diamat').

7. LENIN. HIS LIFE AND HIS ACHIEVEMENTS. Vladimir Il'ič Ulianov, known under the name of 'Lenin', was born on 22 April 1870 – 13 years before Marx died – in Simbirsk on the Volga as the son of a school inspector. He began his studies at the university of Kazan in 1887, a year of reprisals against the revolutionaries. During it Lenin's brother Alexander was executed while he himself, already member of a revolutionary group, was exiled to a village 30 miles distant. However, he was soon allowed to resume his studies. In 1889 he moved to Samara, then to St. Petersburg where he passed his law examination in the same year. In 1892 he became a lawyer; in 1895 he was arrested for illegal activities and exiled to Siberia in 1897. There he married Nadežda Krupskaja in 1898 and began a happy married life. On being freed in 1900 he emigrated abroad. For several years he continued living in various countries abroad, including England and Switzerland. On the outbreak of revolution in 1905 he returned illegally to Russia but was compelled, after its failure, to retire to Finland in 1907. In 1912 he went to Paris and then to Cracow;

27

in 1915 he returned to Switzerland. In 1917 the Germans sent him back to Russia in a sealed railway carriage. He arrived on 17 April, 1917, brought the revolution to a successful end and became the undisputed leader of the country. He died on 21 January 1924, at 6.50 p.m., as can be seen in *Kratkij filosofskij slovar'*. [2]

Among Lenin's numerous works – they amount to 30 volumes – only two are of a purely philosophic character: *Materialism and Empiriocriticism*, which was published by himself in 1909, and the *Philosophical Notebooks*, a collection of notes and essays written during the First World War and published for the first time in 1929 (editor: Adoratsky). But many discussions of philosophical problems are to be found in his political writings as well as in several essays; among them are *The Three Sources and the Three Components of Marxism* (1913) and *The Task of Fighting Marxism* (1922).

8. LENIN. HIS CHARACTER (A SKETCH). Lenin is the real founder of contemporary Dialectical Materialism. His personality left such a powerful imprint on this system that it is necessary to know his character in order to understand this doctrine correctly. He was an astonishingly diverse personality. He was clean living, well mannered, respectable, very modest and very self-sacrificing for his family; but at the same time he was responsible for the mass massacres carried out by the Cheka (amounting to an estimated 1,200,000). He was a man of action, and yet, there have been few others who have felt as strong an inclination towards philosophy. He was a great destroyer – one of the greatest that history has known – but one must not overlook the fact that in his destructive actions he was guided by constructive ideas. Many other antinomies could be noted in his character. But these contradictions disappear and his character becomes understandable if two facts are taken into consideration: he was a man of outstanding ability, and an engineer on a vast scale – a technician of power and of revolution.

Lenin was, as we have just said, a man of great ability. Evidence for this need not be looked for in his activities; the results he achieved, especially in view of the means at his disposal, speak for themselves. But reference must be made to the importance of some of his judgements in the philosophical field. It may be an exaggeration to claim, as G. A. Wetter [3] does, that some day, when Communism will have disappeared, Russia will still owe Lenin a heritage of good principles. Nevertheless, it is true that Lenin perceived a number of truths about his time which scarcely anybody else perceived; for instance, the correctness of realism and of categorial pluralism, the true meaning of reason and much else of importance which we shall have occasion to discuss presently. What is particularly remarkable about him is the fact that he was, at one and the same time, a man of action and a thinker; as a thinker he recognized, with incomparable force, the importance of the philosophic idea – a circumstance which is almost unknown in the case of other great revolutionaries and military leaders.

Above all, however, he was a genius as an engineer and technician. To begin with, Lenin was completely unfettered by ethics and could not see what connection morality might have with social and political action; the latter was, in his eyes, a purely technical field. He displayed the engineer's viewpoint in considering the individual – even the members of his own party – as raw material which he must mould or, at best, use as a tool. The same characteristic expressed itself in his attitude towards the state which, contrary to revolutionary tradition, he revered. Lenin saw the state as an outstanding instrument for action. The emphasis he layed on the denial of God stemmed undoubtedly from the Russian tradition; but this negation, which occupied a central position in his thought, can best be understood by considering him as an engineer who saw in God an impediment to his freedom of action and a dangerous rival; when arguing with his opponents, he generally tried to show that their ideas led to religion – whereupon he would end the discussion. [4] Only by looking at Lenin in this way can one understand how this demagogic revolutionary could be at the same time a thinker. His genius as an engineer also characterized his works; Stalin was perfectly right when he said that Lenin 'americanized' the Russians. It is a fact that Lenin's disciples are far from being the revolutionary dreamers their predecessors were; they are practical technicians; and Leninism has always been a cult of technical practice.

9. LENIN'S PHILOSOPHY. When dealing with contemporary Dialectical Materialism it is necessary to analyze Lenin's thought which, incidentally, will come to the fore again and again; it will suffice if we show what Lenin's original contribution to Marxism has been.

First of all, he *fused into one the doctrines of Marx and Engels*. For him these two thinkers are as one and he always maintained – erroneously – that their views were identical. In practice he almost always followed Engels and saw Marx only as reflected by Engels.

Secondly, he worked out an *epistemology* which was original in many ways. It was essentially a theory, combining pure realism with rationalism, which affirmed the existence of absolute truth; in this theory due regard was paid to the difficulties engendered for realism by the latest results of research in physics. In this field Lenin's doctrine stemmed from his discussions with the Russian followers of E. Mach (1838–1918) and, to some extent, of R. Avenarius (1843–1896) and especially with A. A. Malinovskij (1873–1928) who early in this century, and under the pseudonym 'A. Bogdanov', published a work entitled *Empiriomonism*. This obliged Lenin to study Mach's doctrine. He interpreted it as a subjectivist and sensualist form of idealism and, fighting against it, developed the views mentioned above. *

Thirdly Lenin put special emphasis on the *importance of human will* in the process of social evolution and, by doing so, abandoned, to all intents and purposes, Marx's classical economic determinism. Admittedly these ideas of his were combined with Historical Materialism; but it is the doctrine of will and not Historical Materialism that quite clearly formed the centrepiece of his philosophy. This helps one understand why, contrary to all rules of Marxism, Lenin could preach and achieve a revolution in a country which, according to Marxist doctrine, was least ripe for revolution because least industrialized.

Here Lenin stood much closer to Hegel than to Marx and Engels, although he interpreted the *dialectic* in his own way. For him, too, the 'kernel' of this dialectic lay in the 'unity of opposites' [5]; in the foreground he placed not the unity but the opposites – their struggle and the destruction of the thesis by the antithesis. [6]

A fifth element is connected with the last two: the thesis that this philosophy is *linked to a party,* a thesis which is, it is true, contained in Marx's

---

* It is important to point out that only a one-sided view of Lenin can be obtained through the study of his first philosophical book *Materialism and Empiriocriticism,* in which he develops these ideas. This work contains but few ideas on dialectic, more being found in *Philosophical Notebooks.* That is why the picture of Lenin, given by Harper, is unsatisfactory in spite of all the author's characteristic acuity.

Historical Materialism but which Lenin formulated specifically and with particular sharpness.

Finally, reference must be made to Lenin's attitude towards *religion*. His rejection of religion is not just one of the consequences of materialism and the doctrine of superstructure, as it was for Marx, but one of the logical bases of his philosophy – perhaps the most important one.

In spite of all this, Lenin remained a Marxist and was convinced that he was the only one to have remained true to the master. In actual fact, his Marxism is considerably modified. It was a form of Marxism to which had been added a blend of typically Russian traits and features belonging to Lenin's character, features characteristic of an engineer of genius who went far beyond the framework of the two main doctrines which supplied him with his material.

REFERENCES: [1] Berdyaev 1938, 29 et seq. [2] KFS 133b. [3] Wetter 1948, 395: *'un viatico di buoni principi'*. [4] See for instance ME 181, 208, 227, 357; FT 189, 299. [5] FT 213. [6] Cf. Chapter VIII.

III. THE HISTORY OF PHILOSOPHY IN SOVIET RUSSIA

1. GENERAL OUTLINE AND HISTORICAL BACKGROUND. The history of philosophy in Soviet Russia * can be divided into four periods which correspond almost exactly to the four stages of political development of the country; they are delimited by decrees of the Central Committee of the Bolshevik Party.

The first stage 'war socialism' lasted from the revolution (October 30 1917 old style) till the end of 1921 and was a period of transition. The second stage (1921–1930) began with the exclusion of the non-Leninist

---

* We frequently use the expression 'Soviet Russia' instead of 'Soviet Union' for the following reasons: 1] The Russians are unquestionably the predominant element in Soviet philosophy; the contribution of the other nationalities is quite limited. 2] It is, after all, not a free union but a community of peoples united by force and ruled in the interests of the Russian nation. That this is so is shown by the mere fact that between 1926 and 1939 the Russian population increased by 21 % (from 77.8 to 99 million) while that of the minorities increased by only 7 % (from 69 to 71 million). [1]

philosophers and concluded with the decree condemning Deborin (January 25 1931). It was a period of impassioned discussions about the interpretation of Marxism-Leninism. In the political sphere this was the time of the NEP (from March 1 1921 onwards) and of the struggles among the Bolshevik leaders after Lenin's death (1924). These struggles ended with Stalin's final victory (Trotsky's banishment to Alma Ata in 1929). The third stage (1931–1947) began with the above-mentioned decree and lasted up to the condemnation of G. F. Aleksandrov in 1947. During this period peace reigned and there was a total lack of original stirrings in philosophy – if one excepts the publication of Stalin's *Dialectical Materialism and Historical Materialism* (1938). This was, roughly speaking, the time of the 5-year plans (the first till 1929, the second till 1932) and of the extermination of the anti-Stalin Bolsheviks – after Kirov's assassination (December 1 1934) – achieved in the famous trials (Zinov'ev and Kamenev, August 24, 1935; Radek, January 23–30 1937; Tuxačevskij, 1937; Bukharin, 1938).* It was an age of terrorism which lasted right into the war (invasion of Poland in 1939, attack on Finland in 1940 and war with Germany, 1941–1945). On June 25 1947, a new period began during which can be expected, it would seem, a renewal and intensification of philosophical activity. Whether or not a fifth period began on June, 25 1956 ('demotion' of Stalin) is a question that must be left unanswered.

2. THE FIRST STAGE. From the time when the Party seized power on October 30 1917, and right up to 1921, Russia was suffering from civil war. There was no time for philosophy. As soon as the situation became a little more normal, the Party began to liquidate the non-Bolshevik philosophers. Indeed, in the autumn of 1921 all those university professors who had not fallen victim to the Cheka were relieved of their posts. In the autumn of 1922 the outstanding ones among them – N. Berdyaev, S. Frank, I. Ilyin, N. Lossky – were banished fom Russia, after having suffered repeated arrests. The story is told that Lenin had Ilyin released after reading his book on Hegel; but this did not save him from banishment. Between 1922 and 1930 works by contemporary non-Communist philosophers were published only in exceptional cases [2]; since 1930,

---

* According to moderate estimates the number of death sentences amounted to 6,000.

apparently none at all (apart from a few mathematical-logical works which, however, do not count in this connection). The reactionary ideology had been exterminated; a *tabula rasa* had been created on which a new structure was to be erected.

In fact, when the revolution broke out in Russia there was no shortage of men who were devoting themselves to philosophy. Lenin was now the dictator of the whole country. Apart from him one should mention Lidia I. Axelrod, N. Bukharin, Leon Trotsky and others as people who concerned themselves with philosophy even before the revolution. Lunačarskij became Commissar for Education in the Russian Republic although he had formerly been an opponent of Lenin. Other names could be added to these. In 1921 the Institute of Red Professors had taken up its activities with the stipulation that it should train new university teachers in the Marxist spirit. In 1922 the periodical *Pod Znamenem Marksizma* (Under the Banner of Marxism) began to appear under the editorship of A. M. Deborin. Around this periodical broke out the discussions and quarrels which finally ended with the 1931 decree.

3. STALIN. The man who, owing to his political position, was destined to play a decisive role in the development of philosophy in Soviet Russia was Iosif Vissarionovič Džugašvili – generally known as 'Stalin'. He was born on December 21 1878 in Gori (near Tiflis), the son of a village cobbler; unlike Marx, Engels and Lenin, who belonged to the middle class, Stalin was born in poor circumstances. He attended the village school of the church and, at the age of 15, went to the Orthodox seminary in Tiflis. He was expelled from there in 1899 for revolutionary activities. From 1898 onwards he belonged to the Socialist Party and devoted himself to work for the Party in Tiflis and Baku. He was arrested for the first time in 1902 and it was from prison that he sent his declaration of adherence to the Bolshevik party. Between 1902 and 1917 he was arrested no fewer than six times. In 1917 he took part in the revolution and became a member of the first Politburo (October 27 1917); he remained on it with Lenin, Trotsky and Sverdlov when its membership was reduced to four in 1918. From 1922 onwards he was the secretary of this highest party organ. When Lenin died in 1924, a violent struggle for power broke out among the Bolshevik leaders; this struggle, which lasted for years, ended when Stalin emerged as master of the situation. He had almost all

33

the proved Bolsheviks condemned and executed. From that time, until his death on March 5 1953, Stalin was the unassailable dictator of the whole of Russian life and thought. For almost three years after his death he remained the authority for Communists; he lost this position on February 2 1956 (speech by N. S. Khrushchov).

It is difficult to call Stalin a philosopher; his *opera omnia philosophica* consists all told of half a chapter in the History of the Party (28 pages in the Russian edition of 1947) – itself only a résumé of the principal themes of Marx and Engels as seen through Lenin's eyes – and of some 40 pages of reflections on linguistics (1950). *

In spite of this, Russia and the other Communist countries regarded Stalin as a philosophical genius and it is almost impossible to find a single philosophical publication which does not mention him as that. The reason for this is to be sought partly in the importance which Leninism attaches to the practical element and partly in the attitude of the Russians towards their ruler. But one cannot overlook Stalin's great influence on philosophical thought in the U.S.S.R. This is shown above all in the decrees of condemnation which we will now discuss.

4. THE THREE TRENDS OF PHILOSOPHY. The second period – especially during its last years – was characterized by impassioned discussions on the interpretation of the true foundations of Leninism; they are carried out in the Communist style, i.e. they take the orthodoxy of the doctrine as their point of departure and they are punctuated by denunciations. It is not surprising that there should have been such disputes, for Lenin's Dialectical Materialism contains two mutually exclusive factors: materialism and Hegel's dialectic. And so, in their interpretation of Leninism one group attached more importance to materialism and neglected the dialectic; another group gave particular prominence to the dialectic; meanwhile a third group sought to create a balance between the two elements. Thus there arose three philosophical parties: the 'mechanists', the 'Menshevik idealists', and the 'orthodox' group.

The *mechanists* – among them are Bukharin, Axelrod, Stepanov, Minin – gave Leninism an anti-dialectical interpretation; they retained the concept

---

* *Problems of Leninism* is often cited as a further philosophical work by Stalin. This is a misinterpretation, for this book does not deal with philosophy except in a few marginal comments.

34

of a final state but conceived the changes as being purely quantitative and denied any qualitative difference between the various phases in the evolution of matter. Representatives of this trend also believed in a radical form of determinism which had its root in the concept of the automatic movement of matter *(samotek)*; in sociology they insisted on a naturalistic conception *(stixijnost')* of the evolutionary process. They also tended to deny that philosophy is a science. On the whole, the writers of this group emphasized the materialistic element in Marxism.

At the head of the second group, whom Stalin stigmatized as *'mensheviz-ing idealists'*, stands A. M. Deborin (b. 1881); Leon Trotsky (1879–1940) is also reckoned as belonging to this group. There is no clear-cut distinction between the representatives of this conception and the orthodox Leninists as there is in the case of the 'mechanists'. At their trial they were criticized for using the dialectic as Hegel had used it – i.e. without adapting it to materialism –, for seeing in matter a sum of 'mediations' (Deborin) and finally for underestimating Lenin's originality in philosophy in favour of Plekhanov's. In short, this group was accused of giving a one-sided emphasis to the 'dialectical' element in Marxism. But this accusation does not seem to be properly justified.

Finally the *orthodox group* which was recognized as such by the Party in 1931 should be mentioned. It consisted of the two leaders of the Communist cell of the Institute of Red Professors, M. Mitin and P. Judin; they had V. Ral'čevič as a follower and, after the condemnation of Deborin, all the Communist philosophers. This group tried to harmonize the two elements of the doctrine, its materialism and its dialectic.

5. THE 1931 CONDEMNATION. Up to 1925 the *mechanists,* representing as they did ideas of the average, militant Communist, seemed to be in control of the situation; but in the course of that year a strong opposition arose in the person of Deborin. A discussion ensued; it was carried on partly by the periodical *Under the Banner of Marxism* edited by Deborin. The discussion centered around the question of whether the higher forms of matter (life, mind) can be traced back to the lower without 'leaps' *(skačok)*. The Deborinists carried the day. The publication of Lenin's *Philosophical Notebooks* (1929) gave them new arguments and the second Congress of the Marxist-Leninist Scientific Workers (April 1929) represented a complete victory for Deborin over his opponents.

But Stalin intervened. While rejecting the *mechanists* in a speech to the meeting of Scientist-Agronomists on 27 December 1929, he spoke slightingly of the official philosophers. The Orthodox philosophers now made use of this speech to attack Deborin and his group openly. On 24 April 1930, Deborin scored another victory, but he was already on the defensive. On 9 December 1930, Stalin made another speech in which he described Deborin's tendency as 'menshevizing idealism'. Shortly after, on January 25 1931, his doctrine and the periodical were condemned officially by the highest authority in the country, the Central Committee of the Party. This condemnation was commented on at length in a resolution by the cell of the Institute of Red Professors. When published in *Pravda* on the following day, January 26, accusations were poured over the defeated.

This condemnation shows up the characteristic fact that the two tendencies, which were branded as 'heretical', were both linked to political movements; the mechanists to a right-wing deviation, the Menshevik idealists to a left-wing deviation (Trotskism). On this occasion the Communists once again made it patently clear that in their opinion philosophy and politics are indissolubly linked together; there is no political movement without philosophy and no philosophy which does not act as mouthpiece for a political movement.

Deborin submitted; he even published an article in which he admitted that he had fallen into the depths where the possibility of collaboration between proletarian and bourgeois was recognized [3] – which in fact he had never done. His followers hastened to prove their zeal for the party by heaping abuse on him. But it is not true that he was punished in any other way – apart from being dismissed from the editorship of the periodical.

6. THE SECOND PERIOD: 1931-1947. After the 1931 condemnation there were no more discussions; a united 'front' had been established and everybody taught exactly the same. Productivity in the sphere of philosophy declined. The fundamental works of Communist philosophy belong almost exclusively to the second period; among them are Bukharin's and Deborin's writings, the initiation of the Great and Small Soviet Encyclopedias and the many interesting articles in the review *Under the Banner of Marxism*. Henceforth people were concerned with populariza-

tion; they quoted the 'classics' as often as they could and avoided, as much as possible, all dangerous problems. During this period the specifically Communist philosophical style was developed; a style which was characterized by the frequency of superlatives, especially when mentioning the classics and above all Stalin. A. Ždanov, in his speech to the Philosophers' Congress in 1947, had the following to say of the situation of philosophy in Russia: "Philosophic production is utterly insignificant in quantity and feeble in quality. In fact monographs and philosophical articles have real scarcity value."[4] He added that the Communist philosophers lacked a progressive spirit, that they restricted their discussions to historical problems long since solved and that they were afraid to tackle new questions.[5] Such declarations must always be carefully examined before being accepted, for the Communists are in the habit of exaggerating their self-criticism; but there is no exaggeration in this case. The editors of *Voprosy Filosofii* were perfectly correct in saying, in an article in the second volume, that the great majority of philosophical works in Russia were books for popularizing the doctrine or books on the history of science in the nineteenth century.[6]

M. P. Baskin, a professor of philosophy in Moscow, was even more severe in his judgment: "Comrades, if we disregard the bibliographical studies of philosophical works published in recent years we discover that there have been no philosophical works at all. Of course there exist the great works of Marx, Engels, Lenin and Stalin, but so far we have not produced any works which tackle the concrete problems of the socialist order on the basis of Marxism-Leninism. Comrade Kammari said it was our fault because Comrade Aleksandrov had read our monographs. What monographs is Comrade Kammari thinking about? There have been no monographs."[7] As for the content of the philosophical works, this is what he has to say of them: "We write all our books in the same way and with the same result ... Why? .. Supposing someone writes a really original article which expresses the author's own ideas and which does not conform to the stereotyped forms laid down by the editor, What happens? It is not accepted or, and this is more likely, it is edited in such a way that all its individuality is destroyed; and so all our articles look one like the other."[8]

However, during this period an event took place which had supreme importance for the Bolshevik philosophy; this was the appearance, in

1938, of the *History of the Communist Party* in which half a chapter (IV) and a conclusion were written by Stalin. This chapter, entitled 'On Dialectical and Historical Materialism' is, admittedly, only a summary of the philosophic doctrine of the Party; but, coming from the dictator of Communist thought, it was particularly important in that it gave the whole of this philosophy a more definite course. It must also be said that Stalin succeeded in expressing clearly the substance of Lenin's doctrine. Since then, this text has belonged to the most quoted 'classics', and what is more, it is the principal authority for contemporary Dialectical Materialism.

7. THE 1947 CONDEMNATION. It would seem that after the war Stalin became worried by the situation of Soviet thought, and this for two reasons: on the one hand it appeared to him too passive and, on the other, it took liberties which were incompatible with Soviet democracy. Besides, during the war the national spirit had been particularly fostered; the need was therefore felt to adopt this element officially in the intellectual life of the country. First of all, a declaration of principles was made by the Central Committee of the Party in 1946; these dealt with the 'ideological front' in general. Then it was shown how this declaration applied to various groups of intellectuals. In March 1947, and by order of the Central Committee of the Party [9], a debate was held at the Institute of Philosophy of the USSR Academy of Sciences. It was about G. F. Aleksandrov's *History of Philosophy in Western Europe* (1946). This book took the place of the *History of Philosophy*, a compendium whose third volume had been condemned for underestimating nationalism and overestimating the importance of the German classics. Aleksandrov was rewarded with the Stalin Prize; nevertheless, it was soon resolved to submit both him and the whole of Soviet philosophy to a critical review.

The March discussion, at which fifteen persons participated, was held to be insufficient by the Central Committee. It convened from June 16–25 1947, a congress of more than 90 philosophers under the chairmanship of A. Ždanov (Stalin's son-in-law), an outstanding politician and secretary of the Central Committee of the Party. At this congress the speakers (55 participants spoke) criticized the accused book and, finally, Ždanov himself spoke (June 24). He began by stating that he was not a philosopher; then he criticized Aleksandrov's book sharply as well as the work of Soviet philosophers in general. Aleksandrov was accused of not having understood the nature of Marxism and its relations with the earlier philosophies; of having neglected Russian philosophy; of lacking the fighting spirit of the Party; of not using Lenin's energetic language and of being objective – not to mention his technical errors and considerable lacunae. Ždanov criticized the philosophers in general for isolating themselves from the people, for lacking respect for their readers, for neglecting their contacts with one another and above all for being cowards. By this last accusation he meant that they treated only such problems as involved no risk and that they dared not tackle problems of systematic philosophy which affect the whole of life, for instance, the question of what the nature of the dialectical struggle should be like in a classless society. He named several fields which they should have investigated and demanded that they show more fighting spirit in working out the problems of systematic philosophy.

Ždanov declared that he was speaking in the name of the Central Committee and was commissioned by Stalin himself.[10] The philosophers tried to outdo one another in their condemnations of Aleksandrov and of Soviet philosophy in general. As for Aleksandrov himself, he spoke last and made a stirring speech in which he thanked Ždanov and requested him in the name of all the philosophers present to assure Stalin that they would do their best to fulfil Stalin's demand.[11]

Henceforward Ždanov's speech was considered as a 'near classic' and the discussion itself – published verbatim – as having fundamental importance for the development of Soviet philosophy.[12] This is still true for the fourth edition of the authoritative *Short Philosophic Dictionary* of 1954. [13] Here, in fact, began a new period in the development of this philosophy.

8. THE THIRD PERIOD: SINCE 1947. In some respects this period resembles the first period (1921–1931); above all, in that once again philosophic discussion takes place in Soviet Russia. Admittedly these discussions deal with the correct interpretation of Leninism-Stalinism and they are carried out by methods customary among Communists (quotations from the classics, accusations of heresy, etc.); here, too, there can be no question of freedom for non-Leninist Marxists, let alone for non-Marxists. But within this framework Soviet Russian philosophy has come alive, at any rate by comparison with the 'dead' second period.

Now, too, the most important events are interventions by the authorities and interference by political factors. The following in particular have been decisive: 1] Stalin's intervention in the discussion on linguistics (condemnation of N. J. Marr's application of Marxism to the theory of language, June 20 1950). This led to considerable liberalization in the field of formal logic. 2] Certain other utterances of Stalin's which stimulated some philosophers to put more stress on Lenin's *soznatelnost'*. 3] Stalin's death (1953) did not lead to any further liberalization, as is thought by many in the West; on the contrary, it led to a return to more disciplined orthodoxy which contrasts with Stalin's later utterances. * It is too early to say whether and, if so, to what extent the official condemnation of Stalin by Khrushchov on February 2 1956 – and its extension to the field of science by Mikoyan – will affect the sphere of philosophy.

We shall mention, presently, some of the more detailed points raised in the discussions about logic, psychology, etc. For the moment, to illustrate the new situation, it will suffice to mention the following discussion: immediately after Ždanov's speech a new periodical, *Voprosy Filosofii*, was founded. This periodical was directed by B. M. Kedrov who evidently belonged to a moderate trend. Right at the start (1947) he published an interesting article by M. A. Markov on cognition in the field of microphysics. Markov, quite apart from exhibiting a doctrine which was quite untenable from the Marxist point of view, maintained that the philosophers were not entitled to criticize theories of physics. Kedrov thereupon published an article (1948) in which, with special reference to nationalism, he criticized the 'exaggerations'. Markov was then attacked violently and crudely in the *Literaturnaja Gazeta* by A. A. Maksimov while B. Mitin took up the cudgels for him in the same periodical. [14] The editors of

---

* The following details of the general development are well known. The period lasting from Stalin's death to his 'demotion' can be divided into 3 parts: 1] Continuation of Stalin's policy from his death till March 3 1954. 2] The Aleksandrov period: March 16 1954 to March 3 1955. The philosopher whom Ždanov had attacked was appointed Minister of Culture by Malenkov and initiated a more liberal policy in various fields. 3] The Mixajlov period: in March 1955 Aleksandrov was dismissed in disgrace and replaced by Mixajlov; this began a return to 'stricter discipline' in the above-mentioned sectors. This development is well-illustrated in the field of music (see Schlusser in Moseley: Russia since Stalin); but its effect on philosophy is not demonstrable, at any rate not on the evidence of published matter.

Voprosy defended themselves in a large-scale debate [15] in which they insisted, on the authority of many quotations, that Maksimov and not Markov had been untrue to Leninism. But the mouthpiece of the minister of propaganda, *Kultura i žizn'*, took up a position antagonistic to Kedrov and his group; the editor-in-chief was forced to publish a humiliating letter [16] on November 13 1949, in which he retracted * his 'errors'. Nevertheless he was dismissed from the editorship of *Voprosy*.

This kind of thing happened again and again. What was novel about it all was that such discussions could take place at all; before 1947 they would have been unthinkable.

As regards the period since Stalin's death (1953–1955) G. L. Kline, who made a searching study of this period, did not find anything specially new. The situation seemed to have altered in one of its aspects only, namely in the sphere of the history of philosophy. Here Kline observed more receptivity for Western ideas, at any rate to the extent that Western philosophers were read more. [17] Of course they were read only in order to be refuted; even so, this led to a really unusual event, when in 1953, a philosophic and 'idealistic' book by a contemporary philosopher – Heisenberg's famous work – was published in a Russian translation in Moscow. [18] It is impossible to say yet whether this is a posthumous aftermath of the 'liberalism' of the late Stalin era or the first step towards something really new.

9. DESCRIPTION OF THE CURRENT PERIOD. In its external mani-festations philosophy in Soviet Russia is much more intensively alive than before 1947. The following figures will show this:

Among the eight departments of the Academy of Sciences of the USSR, the department of history and philosophy stands sixth; since 1944 it has been publishing an information journal; to it is attached an Institute of Philosophy which appears to have university status and which trains future professors of philosophy. In 1948 it had 82 students. [19] In the course of 1947 10 dissertations were presented [20]. Apart from this In-stitute there existed, in 1946, faculties of philosophy at only 3 of the 30 universities in the USSR; in Moscow, Leningrad and Kaunas.** [21] It is

---

* One page of this letter is reproduced at the end of this book.
** According to M. T. Iovčuk there were to be only two 'peripheral' *philosophical* institutes *(učreždenija)* ; in the Ukraine and in Azerbaidžan (VF 1947, I, 221a).

known, however, that in Moscow alone, philosophical dissertations were presented at the following institutes: at the Academy of Social Sciences, attached to the Central Committee of the Party (32 dissertations), at the University (11), at the State Pedagogic Institute (2), at the Municipal Pedagogic Institute (10), at the Institute of Economics (1) [22]; 56 all told. This number seems to have shrunk with the passage of years as J. A. Andreev mentions only 13 dissertations for 1953 [23]; in 1953–1954 it is reported that 13 have been printed. [24]

The periodical *Under the Banner of Marxism* ceased publication in 1944 and so, for 3 years, there was no philosophical journal in Soviet Russia.* As has been said already, one of the outcomes of the discussions of June 1947 was the founding of a new journal, *Voprosy Filosofii* (Problems of Philosophy). This appeared first in 2, then in 3 and later in 6, issues a year. This is, it is true, very bulky for a periodical. For instance, the 1955 volume contains 1423 large ($6\frac{1}{2}$ by 10 inches) and closely printed pages – which is more than the bulkiest European periodical of this kind, *Tijdschrift voor Philosophie*. *Voprosy Filosofii* published articles on systematic philosophy, studies on the history of philosophy (especially of Russian philosophy), violent attacks against this or that contemporary philosopher (e.g. Carnap, Dewey, Eddington, Marcel, Maritain, Russell), book reviews and a voluminous chronicle.

But the quantity of philosophical production seems still to be rather meager. After all, *Voprosy* is the only philosophical journal in the USSR **, a country of 160 million inhabitants, whereas there are 16 such journals in the U.S.A. This periodical mentioned only 9 philosophical books in 1948 while *Mind* alone, for instance, contains reviews of 46 books.

In accordance with Ždanov's instructions, great projects have been planned since 1947. The Academy of Sciences was to publish no less than 40 volumes [25]; in fact, the number of philosophical books published does seem to be slightly higher than 10 years ago. Thus a list of books in this field published in 1955 contained 41 titles (13 reprints or translations, 8 systematic studies – mostly handbooks – and 20 historical studies). [26]

---

* In 1946 and in 1948 respectively there appeared one number of the *Filosofskie Zapiski;* they scarcely qualify as a periodical.
** See footnote on p. 70.

REFERENCES: [1] Lorimer; Zabuski. [2] List of titles in Kline 1952, 128. [3] Danzas 436. [4] Žd 267a. [5] Žd 268a. [6] VF 1947, 2, 7. [7] VF 1947, 1, 159. [8] VF 1947, 1, 161. [9] Ždanov in VF 1947, 1, 4. [10] Žd. 267a. [11] VF. 1947, 1, 288 et seq. See appendix. [12] Pr 326a. [13] KFS (4) 167 et seq. [14] 9. 3. 1949. Extracts in Schlesinger 2. [15] *Diskussija po prirode*, VF 1948, 4, 203–234. [16] See Schlesinger 1; Cf. Appendix. [17] Kline 1956, 138. [18] CF. VF 1955, 1, 189–195. [19] VF 1948, 2, 369a. [20] VF 1947, 2, 373. [21] Learned World 1947. [22] VF 1947, 2, 372 et seq. [23] VF 1954, 3, 201. [24] VF 1955, 6, 262. [25] Vasil'ev. [26] VF 1956, 3, 254.

IV. EXTERNAL CHARACTERISTICS AND SPIRIT

Before presenting the doctrine of Dialectical Materialism itself it is essential to find out its spirit as well as the characteristics which distinguish it from Western philosophies. These characteristics can be classified as follows: philosophy is considered as being of the utmost importance; it acknowledges certain 'classical' texts and accepts their content as *the* truth and as being above discussion; its development is strictly supervised by the Party; the attitude of its representatives is extremely dogmatic and polemical; they use an entirely different language from that used by Western philosophers; finally they profess extreme nationalism in philosophy. Most of these characteristics which can be deduced from what was said in Chapter II, we shall attempt to explain systematically later on. We shall begin by describing them.

I. IMPORTANCE OF PHILOSOPHY IN COMMUNISM. The Communists regard philosophy as a matter of fundamental importance; in this they differ from the majority of those in the West whose thought has been influenced by positivism.

Indeed, as C. E. M. Joad puts it so well, [1] Communism is 'philosophy in action'. Lenin taught that "there can be no revolutionary movement . . . without a revolutionary theory." [2] Now this theory is founded on the Communist conception of the world which is identical with Dialectical Materialism. That is why "Dialectical and Historical Materialism forms the theoretical foundation of Communism and of the Marxist party . . . and (that is why) it is the duty of every active fighter in our party to assimilate it." [3] All contemporary Soviet philosophers subscribe to this thesis of Stalin: for instance, almost all those who spoke in the great debate of 1947, Stepanjan [4], Leonov [5], Kalinin [6], Rozental' [7], Aleksandrov. [8] Ždanov even claims that the "composition of a handbook on the history of philosophy is a matter of supreme importance." [9]

This *theory* particularly stresses the dependence of the sciences on the principles of this philosophy, [6] both as to content and as to method. Thus, in Soviet Russia numerous scientific doctrines were condemned because the Party organs declared them incompatible with the teachings of their philosophy.

Practice corresponds to theory. Philosophy is taught on a vast scale. For instance, in 1945 the curriculum for activists envisaged as many as 126 hours of philosophy out of a total of 340. [10] A course of studies at the Institute of Agriculture included 240 hours of chemistry and 100 hours of Dialectical Materialism. * [11] Works of philosophy are published in vast editions in the Soviet Union. According to Mitin [14] 327,000,000 copies of the works of Marx, Engels, Lenin and Stalin had been distributed in 22 years (by September 1 1952, this number had risen to 931,536,000, including 32,775,000 copies in foreign languages [15]). Meanwhile the editions of the works of other philosophers run to the following totals (in thousands): Aristotle 78.3; Voltaire 228.6; Hegel 200.5; Diderot 139.1; Spinoza 55.2; Feuerbach 44; Bacon 23; Holbach 79.4; Helvetius 67.5; Democritus 10. *The History of the Communist Party*, containing the chapter by J. Stalin, reached a distributed total of 35,762,000, of which 27,567,300 copies). ** [17] In positivist Europe the Bolsheviks publish a great number of philosophical works for purposes of propaganda; the *Editions Sociales Françaises* were particularly active in doing this. [18] Finally, philosophy has a great *political importance* which, to all intents and purposes, leads the Communists to identify every philosophy with a political party and

* The same can be observed in other Communist states. Here a few examples: in 1951 the students of the Institute of Medicine and Pharmacology in Bucharest had to devote 6 hours a week in their first year and 11 in their second year to lectures on Marxism-Leninism. [12] In East Germany the Ministry for People's Education decreed that university students should follow a 'basic course of sociological study' which provided for 1,782 hours of philosophy. [13]

** It does not follow that the educated Soviet public is particularly interested in philosophy. On the contrary, conversations with authors from Soviet countries have shown that a normal Russian generally considers philosophy as something dangerous – and rightly so.

every political party with a philosophy. This was, for instance, the case with the *mechanists* and the *Deborinists* in 1930–1931 (cf. Chapter III, 5). Various philosophical principles – for instance the theory of the dialectical 'leap' *(skačok)* – are applied in practice – even against factual evidence, while the enormous importance which is attached to philosophy is shown by the strict *control* which the party exercises over it.

2. THE 'CLASSICS'. The works of Marx, Engels, Lenin and Stalin (until early 1956) – and these alone – play an exceptional part which can be characterized as follows:

a) They are never questioned. Every effort is made to discover their exact meaning and to apply these doctrines to particular cases, but there is never, not even in a marginal comment, the slightest criticism of these authors.

b) They serve as evidence in a discussion. If a Communist philosopher can prove that the doctrine expounded by another philosopher does not agree down to the minutest detail with that of these authors, that is the end of the discussion. Anyone who is attacked tries to prove that his point of view is the same as that of the 'classics'.

c) Until recently it was regarded as a duty to quote these 'classics' constantly. In 1935 the translator of a work by P. Tannery on the history of science was criticized because he had quoted neither Engels nor Marx, neither Lenin nor Stalin in the introduction. [20] Berdyaev tells [21] of an author who was condemned because, in a book on totemism, he had not quoted Lenin – although he assured everybody that Lenin had never written a single word on this subject. And so the philosophical works of the Communists are full of quotations from the 'classics'. Stalin himself gave the lead: in the first 10 pages of his essay he gave no fewer than 18 such quotations, some of them of considerable length. Although there has been a recent decline of rigour in this matter, nevertheless, it is impossible to find a work on philosophy without quotations from the 'classics'. *

d) And so the work of the philosophers in the Soviet Union consists

---

* Sharp protests against this 'quotation mania' *(citatologia, citatnij podxod)* were made during the June 1947 discussion, especially by V. A. Čagin (VF 1, 200b) and M. P. Baskin (160a). Thereupon Ždanov apologized (256a) for having to quote all the same; and this is done not only by him but by almost all other writers, even after the 'discussion'.

almost entirely in writing commentaries on the 'classics' and in discovering how to apply their doctrine to the situation of the moment. *

3. CONTROL BY THE PARTY. The Party exerts an extremely strict control over science and literature in the Soviet Union. It is particularly strict with philosophy. In fact, the following can be said:

a) Since 1922 scarcely a single work by a living philosopher who is not a Marxist-Leninist has been published. This situation, unique in the annals of philosophy, is due *inter alia* to the fact that the state, which is controlled by the Party, is the owner of all printing works, publishing houses, newspapers, etc. and that this Party considers philosophy as an outstanding weapon in the political struggle.

b) Furthermore, the Central Committee of the Party strictly controls the interpretation even within the framework of Marxist-Leninist philosophy. This Committee has even taken several official decisions; for instance on January 25 1931, (against Deborin), on November 11 1938, (on the *History of the Communist Party*), on May 1 1944 (on the errors of the philosophers) and on June 25 1947 (against Aleksandrov).[22] Besides, the minister responsible for higher education in the Russian Republic prohibited logical formalism in a decree dated March 23 1948[23]; the Armenian Central Committee did likewise with the works of V. Xačojan and A. Adamjan in November 1947.[24]

c) Many of the condemnations of representatives of various branches of learning which are pronounced by the same committee or by its organs are based on philosophical arguments. Under this heading are the idealistic tendencies of the ethnographers in 1932 [25], of the anti-realistic writers in 1934 [26], of the so-called 'Pedologues' in 1936 [27], of the intellectuals in general in 1946 [28], of the Mendelian biologists who were rebuked for their 'idealism' in 1948 [29], of certain historians in 1950 [30], of linguists in 1950 [31] and of physiologists in 1950–1951. [32]

* This point was raised particularly often in the 1947 discussion. B. A. Fingert even says that there are very few philosophers in Soviet Russia, i.e. original thinkers (VF 1, 462a). Z. A. Kamenskij points to the difference between the heads of the other scientific institutes and Mitin, Judin, Svetlov, Vaseckij who were successive heads of the Institute of Philosophy: while the others, according to him, are original, creative men, this is what he has to say of the philosophers: "Try and name even one of their works which opens a new page in the science of philosophy, which is an original contribution to philosophy." (VF 1, 377a). "We are bogged down in commenting" admits M. A. Leonov.

This kind of control, with its particular methods *, has had two results which are both very characteristic of contemporary philosophy in the USSR: complete uniformity and a characteristic atmosphere in discussion. In questions of any importance all Communist philosophers have only one opinion, whether they refer to history of philosophy or to systematic philosophy. In this the philosophical publications in the Soviet Union resemble their ballot papers which, as is well known, are almost equally uniform and unanimous.

A further consequence of the control exerted manifests itself in the character of any discussion that takes place in Soviet Russia; pertinent arguments are replaced by accusations of disloyalty towards the 'classics'.The accused authors, in their turn, try to prove the congruence of their views with those of Marx, Engels, Lenin and Stalin; if they are condemned,they admit their guilt and promise to reform while their erstwhile comrades shower accusations upon them. ** After his condemnation, A. Deborin declared publicly that he had 'sunk as low as the filthy depths of the idea which holds that collaboration is possible between proletarian and bourgeois' (which, incidentally, he had never done [33]). In the appendix four similar and recent recantations are given.

* Philosophers and scientists who submit to the resolutions of the Central Committee are not killed, as is often thought in the West. Deborin, for instance, although condemned in 1931, continued to be active as a philosopher; similarly Aleksandrov who, after his condemnation in 1947, was again publishing works as early as 1948 (cf. Bibliography). But this is not the general rule. Ju. Ždanov was expelled from the party in spite of his abject *mea culpa*. As for thinkers who did not submit, severe punishments seem to have been meted out to them. There is one case of this nature: Nikolai Ivanovič Vavilov, an outstanding biologist, was sentenced to be sent to the Kolyma horror camps where he died in 1942 (Dobžanskij, Czapski 211 et seq., Langdon 114 et seq.). A. Kolman declared at the 10th Philosophic Congress at Amsterdam that Vavilov had been an 'English spy' and had admitted it before his death (Hook, 1949, 267), but this does not mean anything; it is all too well known that the victims of the Soviet police admit everything that they are required to (cf. Gitermann 1938; Dallin-Nikolaevskij, Mora).
** As examples we can mention, *inter alia,* the speeches of O.V. Traxtenberg (VF 1, 175 et seq.), Z. V. Smirnova (109 et seq.), V. F. Asmus (276 et seq.) and V. I. Svetlov (54 et seq.) who had all read and approved G. F. Aleksandrov's book and who, nevertheless, attacked him violently during the 1947 'discussion'. See on this the observations by M. P. Baskin (VF. 1, 158b) and P. E. Vyšinskij (227b).

4. THE POLEMICAL AND AGGRESSIVE ATTITUDE. The most striking characteristic of present-day Bolshevik philosophy is the excessively polemical and aggressive attitude of its representatives. Lenin was extremely combative, especially in his ME; in 1921 he even wrote specifically 'On the role of Fighting Materialism'[34]. In this his disciples followed the master faithfully and when, in time, they became rather milder, A. Ždanov was commissioned by Stalin to remind the Communist philosophers of their duty to be polemical and combative. He stated: "The violence and intolerance which Marxism-Leninism has never ceased displaying in its fight against all enemies of materialism is well known ... The model for the Bolshevik fight against all enemies of Marxism is still Lenin's book, *Materialism and Empiriocriticism,* where every word hits the enemy like an annihilating sword-stroke." [35] Similar utterances are numerous in Soviet philosophical literature: there is a constant mentioning of the 'philosophical front', 'strokes', 'shots', etc. Inspired by Ždanov's above-mentioned appeal, numerous articles dealing with this subject appeared; philosophers were urged repeatedly to be fighters. In 1948 alone, four such articles appeared. A large proportion of the philosophical works of the Communists are directed against this or that philosopher or this or that philosophical tendency. One's own attitude is attributed to the philosophers whom one attacks; they are said to have taken orders from capitalist organizations, from the Vatican, from the American government, etc. Communist philosophy today considers itself as an instrument of political warfare and, similarly, considers every other philosophy as such an instrument.

To illustrate this point yet further, here are a few titles of recent philosophical studies, published in 1948: 'Philosophy of Life as an Ideological Weapon of Imperialistic Reaction in China'[36]; 'The Philosophy of Militant Catholicism'[37]; 'Racial Theories in the Service of American Imperialism'[38]; 'Against Formalism and the Unpolitical Attitude in the Theory of Logic'[39]; 'Against Idealism and Metaphysics in the Theory of Heredity'[40]; 'Against Idealist Propaganda'[41]; 'Against the Cringing Attitude Towards Bourgeois Philosophy'[42]. Let it be noted that this refers to studies published in an academic journal, not to works of popularization or of propaganda. Their contents correspond to their titles.

5. DOGMATISM. This philosophy is founded on undisputed, unimpeach-

able texts, it is controlled by an authority which is considered infallible and its function is to be an instrument in the political struggle. It is natural therefore, that this philosophy should be dogmatic. Its representatives in their writings are far less concerned with solving problems than with teaching the solutions already found by the 'classics' and refuting opinions which contradict them. It might be said that the Communist philosophers are not so much seekers or explorers as apostles of a doctrine which is already there. Not only have they a firmly established opinion in regard to all great problems of philosophy, but they also make very little effort to justify and prove it. The critical spirit, as it is understood by Western philosophers, seems to be totally unknown to them. What they understand by 'criticism' and 'self-criticism' is merely the testing of their own or of somebody else's doctrine for loyalty or disloyalty to the theses of the 'classics'. This attitude is expressed, in a remarkably outspoken way, in the preface to Lenin's *Materialism and Empiriocriticism*. As a reply to his critics, who set themselves the task of searching for truth, he said: "As for me, I am also a seeker in philosophy. Indeed, in the papers which follow I have set myself the task of finding out what madness it is that has brought people so far as to serve up, under the guise of Marxism, such incredibly confused, entangled and reactionary stuff." [43] In other words, Lenin does not seek to understand whether Marxism is true; he would rather find out wherein lies the disloyalty of those whom he attacks; i.e. wherein they deviate from established truth. An even more revealing passage is to be found in a letter (printed in the same volume [44]) in which he declared that the very moment he set to work he forgot all about philosophy, wishing to use it only to combat his opponents more successfully. This is the attitude which is characteristic of Communist philosopher.

The same dogmatism is, remarkably enough, to be observed in the history of philosophy. Not only have Communist philosophers their ready-made and perfectly uniform judgment of every philosopher of the past, but even their appreciation of the purely historical importance of a doctrine is dogmatically determined by what the 'classics' have to say about it. Lenin admired Aristotle and valued Plato but little; therefore Aristotle is always the great philosopher while Plato is almost ignored. During the early nineteenth century, mediaeval philosophy was still almost universally held to be fairly unimportant; the views of Communist historians reflect this attitude even today; and so, in order to be faithful to the 'classics' down to the last detail, these historians find themselves in curious opposition to the Marxist theory of evolution. According to this theory Scholasticism should be more – not less – important than ancient philosophy, because it represents a more advanced evolutionary era, namely feudalism. A number of similar examples could be quoted. *

6. THE PHILOSOPHICAL STYLE. The style of the philosophical writings in Soviet Russia reflects these features: pre-eminence of the 'classics', submissiveness to the decision of the Party, aggressiveness and dogmatism. This style is characterized by three further features: it uses a special vocabulary based on superlatives when talking of the 'classics' or of important politicians, and on insults, when talking of opponents. On this score the entire literary production of Communist philosophers contrasts completely in style to that of Western philosophers and strikes a non-Communist reader as repellent.

a) The 'classical' terminology, which has been conditioned by certain historical circumstances and which is sometimes due to an astonishing ignorance of these 'classics', has been fixed once and for all in Communist philosophy. Its usage is occasionally diametrically opposed to that of the West. For instance, 'materialism' for the Communist often means the same as 'realism' for others; thus Aristotle is a materialist. On the other hand, every philosopher who does not represent extreme realism or who rejects materialism is described as being 'idealistic'; thus A. Comte becomes the leader of European 'idealists'[45] – as does J. Maritain who is a realist in the Western sense of the word. [46] 'Historical' is replaced by 'dialectical'; 'contrary' by 'contradictory'; 'positive' and 'good' by 'revolutionary' and 'progressive'. That is why the Western reader who is unfamiliar with this terminology often finds great difficulty in correctly understanding the works of these philosophers.

b) The 'classics' and, above all, the living political leaders are spoken of only in superlatives; in a manner which is customary with many other Eastern nations. They are 'geniuses', 'incomparable leaders', 'thinkers who inaugurate a new epoch', etc. In every Communist philosophical

* Further examples of this attitude will be found in Appendix II.

work that we know, Stalin was described, right up to his death, as the great, the incomparable philosopher of genius, the voice of truth. [47] These epithets strike the Westerner as being nothing but base toadying.

c) On the other hand these same writings teem with insults when dealing with opponents. Lenin calls his opponents' philosophy 'senseless chatter', 'gibberish'[48], 'declamation'[49], 'feeble sophistry'[50], 'boundless stupidity'[51], 'insanity'[52], 'brainlessness'[53], etc.; as for the opponents themselves he calls them 'men without a conscience'[54]; 'muddle-headed professors'[55], 'sophists'[56], 'charlatans'[57], 'flea crackers'[58], 'Philistines'[59], 'agents of the theologians'[60], 'professorial clowns'[61], 'jesters'.[62] A. Ždanov criticized G. F. Aleksandrov for using too polite a style and demanded a return to Lenin's virile language. [63] Samples of this 'virile' style abound in all the writings of Soviet philosophers. In the single 1948 issue of the journal *Voprosy Filosofii*, published by the USSR Academy of Sciences, L. Blum is described as a 'philosophic mercenary of imperialism'[64], E. Gilson and J. Maritain as 'obscurantists', J.P. Sartre and A. Malraux as 'de Gaulle's lackeys'[65], and Eddington as a 'thrall of clericalism'.[66] Examples could be quoted *ad infinitum*.

7. NATIONALISM. A recent feature of Soviet philosophy is an extreme nationalism. Two conventional epithets, applied to those whose attitude is insufficiently chauvinistic, are 'cosmopolitism' and 'servility' *(niskopo-klonstvo)*; they are considered crimes. Thus, for instance, M. M. Rozental' believes that the struggle against them is one of the principal tasks of Soviet aesthetics [67]; an author signing himself 'K.V.' demanded a general campaign against these errors; M. B. Mitin, who is regarded as the outstanding philosopher, violently attacked a fairly moderate article by B. Kedrov because the latter had criticized the ridiculous exaggerations of chauvinism. [68] One can obtain some idea of the extent of this nationalism if one realizes that Aleksandrov himself was condemned because he attributed too much importance to Western philosophers. It was the same Aleksandrov who wrote: "Apart from Marx and Engels, the nineteenth and twentieth centuries have no philosophers who can be compared to Herzen and Belinskij, Černyševskij and Dobroljubov, Plekhanov... let alone Stalin and Lenin'. [69] This attitude also reveals itself in the fact that a certain M. I. Karinskij (1740–1817), the author of a text-book on logic, is praised as one of the greatest of logicians. [70] Let us finish by

51

giving, in brief, the headings of chapters in the historical section of a project for a course on aesthetics [71]: 1. Antiquity, 2. Renaissance, 3. Seventeenth and eighteenth centuries, 4. Germany, 5. Russia in the nineteenth century, 6. Belinskij, 7. Černyševskij, 8. Dobroljubov, 9. Marx and Engels, 10. Plekhanov, 11. Lenin and Stalin. In other words, half the chapters are devoted to Russian 'thinkers on aesthetics'.

This phenomenon is not restricted to philosophy but is typical of all present-day Russian publications.

8. THE 'THEOLOGICAL' CHARACTER. All non-Communist philosophers who have studied this philosophy have been struck by its – admittedly inverted – theological character. This is true, for instance, of B. Russell [72], W. Gurian [73], G. Miche [74], G. A. Wetter [75] and above all of Berdyaev who investigated this problem particularly thoroughly. [76] Indeed, there are to be found all the characteristic features of a theology: 'a Book' as the basis for a doctrine and a 'church' to supervise its interpretation; there is 'orthodoxy' and 'heresy'; official decisions are taken against 'heresies' and finally there is an 'inquisition' to punish the 'heretics'. These features have nothing to do with the value of the results obtained by these writers. According to Whitehead, the discussion of Christian theologians about the Trinity were of fundamental importance for philosophy. It is worth noting that various mediaeval theological analyses contributed to the progress of philosophy. A theologian can be equally at home in the history of philosophy and in philosophy itself; he can carry out perfectly exact and scientific investigations, as has happened, for instance, in Catholic theology, in Mohammedanism and in Indian Buddhism. However, this does not alter the fact that theology is not philosophy; for philosophy, by its very nature, cannot be bound by any authority.

These distinctions are of fundamental importance to the frequently discussed problem of whether or not contemporary Dialectical Materialism is a philosophy. When G. A. Wetter [77] maintains that the principal representatives of Dialectical Materialism in Russia today are well acquainted with philosophy, he concluded from this that they must necessarily be regarded as philosophers. We cannot subscribe to this opinion. It may be true that philosophic training is excellent in the Soviet Union – though even this is doubtful especially in regard to systematic philosophy – but from this one can only deduce that the representatives of Dialectical Materialism know philosophy and not that they are necessarily themselves philosophers – at any rate not in the Western meaning of the word.

One must not overlook one fundamental difference between Christian theology and Communist 'philosophy'. For the Christian the Scriptures are God-inspired; they are the divine word. Whether one believes this or not, one cannot deny that once this belief is accepted it is perfectly logical to attribute infallibility to the Scriptures and, as the Catholics do, to the Church as a divine institution. On the other hand, Communist philosophers do not attribute any divine inspiration or support to their 'classics' and their Central Committee; their works and decisions are, in the eyes of the Communists, absolutely human – which not only radically alters the situation, but also makes it quite incomprehensible for the Western European.

Nothing has come to light in the most recent publications which might be interpreted as revealing a substantial change in these fundamental attitudes. Since Stalin's declaration of 1950, much has been said about the need for free discussion and Lenin's statement, "our theory is not a dogma but an introduction to action", [78] is being quoted constantly (just as it had been earlier). But, in fact, it has been affirmed quite recently, both clearly and authoritatively, that this does *not* apply to the foundations of Marxism-Leninism, i.e. to the real foundations of the philosophy. Thus *Kommunist* (July 1955) published a lead-article which was anonymous and which, therefore, expressed the Party viewpoint: "It is not permissible for individuals to make use of the freedom of discussion and of criticism to revise the fundamental principles". [79] Elsewhere, in the same 'theoretical' organ of the Party, we read: "Within Marxist philosophy there can be no question of different ideological tendencies existing" [80] (from the Marxist point of view), "all 'theories' which contradict Marxism must be branded as such and may not be brought up for discussion". [81]

And so the 'classics' continue to be quoted and used as arguments (except for Stalin who is no longer a 'classic') and the Party continues to make decisions on philosophical questions. Even the 'demotion' of Stalin is one more example of an intervention similar to the old ones. True, the tone has become more polite; but the dogmatic attitude remains and the philosophic style has scarcely altered.

REFERENCES: [1] Joad 607. [2] *Was tun?* In: LAW I. 194 (LSW 4(2), 152). [3] DM 141. [4] In: Dial. Mater. 1947. 3 et seq. [5] Očerk 1948. 46. [6] *Üb. Komm. Erziehung* 1951. 26 et seq. [7] M. dial. Meth. 1954. 9, and Dial. Mat. (Ents.). 3 et seq. [8] Dial. Mat. 1954. 3 et seq. [9] Žd 256a. [10] Miche 125 et seq. [11] Delbos. L'expérience 1933. [12] News from behind the Iron Curtain. June 1952. [13] No. 23 of August 4, 1951, according to Möbus 13 et seq. [14] Mitin 1943. [15] *Sovetskaja Kniga,* October 1952. [16] Zelenov 90, see also Wetter 1948, 217. [17] Struve 111. [18] Kanapa. [19] See below, par. 3. [20] Miche 115. [21] Berdyaev 1934, 64. [22] See above, Chapter 3. [23] See below chapter 5; Osmakov. [24] VF 1947, 2, 384. [25] Laserson II, 702. [26] Struve 235. [27] Tomaševskij 10. [28] VF 1947, 1, 172. [29] *O polozenii,* cf. Langdon-Davies and below, Chapter IX. [30] Vestnik Ak. Nauk No. 11, Nov. 1950. [31]. Pravda 9, 16, 23 and 30 May, 6, 13, 18 June 1950. [32] Pravda 24. July 1951. [33] Danzas 436. [34] Lenin 1922. [35] Žd. 201. [36] VF 1948, 1, 250 et seq. [37] German. [38] Močalin. [39] Vyšinskij. [40] Gluščenko. [41] K.V. [42] Mičurineč. [43] ME S. XXX. [44] ME S XII. [45] KFS⁴, 250a. [46] German. [47] See, for instance, in *'Diskussija po knige'* among others: 19a, 63b, 80a, 121a, 149b, 157, 159, 166b, 178b; see also Miche 77 et seq. [48] ME 133. [49] ME 120. [50] ME 32. [51] ME 326. [52] ME 126. [53] ME 31. [54] ME 84. [55] ME 86. [56] ME 126. [57] ME 135. [58] ME 95. [59] ME 358. [60] ME 351. [61] ME 118. [62] ME 322. [63] Žd 201. [64] VF 1948, 1.233, [65] VF 1948, 2, 279. [66] VF 1948, 2, 287. [67] Rozental' 1948(2). [68] See above chap. 3. [69] As quoted by Feuer 122. [70] Popov, Tavanec. [71] Berestnev. [72] Russell 73. [73] Gurian 1932, 211. [74] Miche 7. [75] Wetter 1948, 226. [76] 1934, 2. [77] Wetter 1948, 78. [78] *Der linke Radikalismus* 8, LAW II, 716. [79] *O diskussijax o naučnyx* ... 119. [80] Id. 123. [81] Kommunist 1955, No. 5 22 et seq.

SYSTEMATIC SECTION

V. DEFINITION AND CLASSIFICATION
OF PHILOSOPHY

I. CONCEPTION OF THE WORLD, SCIENCE AND PHILOSOPHY: MEANING OF THE WORD. The conception of the world (*mirovozzrenie*) was formerly defined as "the all-embracing consideration of all phenomena in nature and society"[1]; or as "a certain system of considering nature and society." [2] A new definition runs as follows: "A system of views (*vzgljadov*), notions and conceptions of the world as a whole." [3] It is often said that Dialectical Materialism, i.e. this philosophy, is the Communist conception of the world [4]; however, a distinction should be drawn between the general and the particular meaning of the term. "The essential kernel of every conception of the world, the conception of the world in the proper sense of the word, is formed by philosophical notions." [5] But interpreted more widely, the conception of the world includes not only philosophy, but also the other sciences. Science has the task of presenting 'an exact chart of the world'; in its wider interpretation, science is a system of apprehending the laws (*zakonomernosti*) which govern nature, human society and thought [6]; while natural science studies the laws of nature, social sciences investigate the laws governing the evolution of human society. [7]

In the ancient world philosophy was identified with science in general; bourgeois philosophy called it the 'science of sciences'. This latter view is rejected as erroneous [8]: philosophy must not be a science ruling over the others. It is an "instrument of scientific investigation, a method which penetrates all sciences, both natural sciences and social sciences." [9] People have tried to deduce from this formulation of Ždanov that philosophy is exclusively a method; nothing but logic, dialectic and epistemology. [10] This may be what Ždanov thinks, but it is certainly not the official doctrine; all official statements give another interpretation of philosophy. For instance the *Decisions of the Theoretic Front* of January 25 1931 [11], stated that philosophy has a goal of its own. Stalin, for his part, attributed to Dialectical Materialism a content apart from method. [12] Elsewhere philosophy is defined as "the science of the most general laws of nature, of human society and of thought" [13]; this latter definition is the one which was accepted in the 1948 Programme. [14] The official doctrine, laid down in 1931, opposed the mechanical materialists (who regarded philosophy as a synthesis of the sciences) and the Deborinists (who were criticized for making philosophy a general methodology). Let us just add that, according to Lenin, philosophy gives the sciences a 'solid foundation' without which no science and no materialism is fit for battle. [15]

It follows that philosophy is an inclusive theory of being (*des Seins*); i.e. it includes metaphysics, ontology and logic (including methodology). But the Communists do not use these terms. As we shall see, presently, they use the concepts 'materialism' (for 'metaphysics' or 'ontology') and 'dialectic' (for 'logic'). Now, as Dialectical Materialism coincides exactly with just these metaphysics, ontology and logic, one should be able to deduce that philosophy and Dialectical Materialism are identical. But it must not be forgotten that in Soviet Russia the actual philosophical doctrine is always divided in two; Dialectical Materialism and Historical Materialism. Stalin describes their relationship thus: "Dialectical Materialism is the conception of the world of the Marxist-Leninist Party... Historical Materialism is the application of the teachings of Dialectical Materialism to the study of the life of society..." [16] This formula has been adopted in the Party programme. It would seem therefore that, according to the Communists, the sciences are built up as shown in the following diagram:

Dialectical Materialism

Historical Materialism

natural sciences

social sciences

We shall now investigate Dialectical Materialism; but we shall also deal briefly with Historical Materialism, for, as we have observed already, the two are intimately connected.

2. CLASSIFICATION OF DIALECTICAL MATERIALISM ACCORDING TO STALIN. In a text which is accepted as authoritative, Stalin analyses the essential components of Dialectical Materialism as follows: "This conception of the world is called Dialectical Materialism because its approach to the phenomena of nature,... its method of apprehending these phenomena, is *dialectical*, and because in its interpretation and conception of natural phenomena its theory is *materialistic*."

58

According to Stalin the dialectical method has four essential features:
a) "... the dialectic views nature... as a coherent, homogeneous entity in which the objects and their appearances are organically linked together..."[18]

b) "... the dialectic views nature... as a state of constant movement and change..."[19]

c) "... the dialectic views the process of evolution... as an evolution... in which qualitative changes occur not gradually but rapidly, suddenly,... not fortuitously but according to certain laws..."[20]

d) "... the dialectic starts from the fact that inner oppositions are immanent in all things in nature and in their appearances...."[21] Therefore, the 'dialectical' element contains, according to Stalin, four theses: nature is an entity, nature evolves, this evolution is inevitable, it takes place in 'leaps' and is caused by the oppositions immanent in things.
Materialism is far from being just a method; it is the 'theory' of the doctrine and has three 'fundamental features':
Philosophic materialism takes as its point of departure the following facts:
a) "... that the universe is by its very nature *material* and that the varied appearances in it are various forms [22] of matter in movement..."

b) "... that matter, nature and being *(das Sein)* represent objective reality which exists outside consciousness and independently of it..."[23]

c) "... that our knowledge of laws of nature... is reliable knowledge..., that there is nothing in the world which cannot be apprehended..."[24]

As was to be expected, this classification is still generally valid. When M. Leonov and M. Rozental' used it in their 1947 works they were praised by V. I. Sviderskij[25]. The 1948 programme which, as a result of the discussion, was to provide the basis for instruction in all higher educational establishments, rigorously followed this classification while making only two additions in each chapter: at the beginning of each, a paragraph described the 'scientific character' of the subject to be treated and, at the end, another paragraph described its 'tremendous practical importance'. [26] The situation seems scarcely to have changed – even since the rejection of Stalin; as late as March 1956 the rector of the University of Tiflis was dismissed for not having fostered the training in Marxism-Leninism with sufficient energy. This training was to be done according to the 1948 'Programme', i.e. according to the classification given above.

3. CRITICISM OF STALIN'S CLASSIFICATION. The contents of Stalin's article which establishes the classification has been drawn almost entirely from Lenin's works. Indeed, even when quoting Marx and Engels, Stalin usually took the quotations from Lenin; and Stalin seems to have succeeded in establishing clearly what was essential in his master's teaching. Unfortunately, he was much less successful in classifying the content; the classification which was his own work, is untenable from the logical point of view of the system.

First of all, what Stalin calls 'dialectical method' is not a method at all but a number of ontological and cosmological theses. He goes out of his way to introduce each of the four theses of the supposed 'dialectical method' with the words, 'the dialectic views..., considers..., from the point of view of dialectic'; by doing so he pretends that he is developing a doctrine on the *manner of considering objects* – which would be a methodology – and not on the *actual nature of the objects* under consideration. It can be claimed that some of the theses of this sequence could make the foundation for a methodology, but all this does not alter the fact that the very nature of his theses clearly shows that they deal with the nature of the universe and not with the manner of considering it. In fact, they are ontological theses. Stalin not only demanded that one should *view* nature in a certain pre-determined manner, he also demanded that one should find that nature *is* actually this or that, that it is an entity, that it is involved in a process of evolution and that it has such and such characteristic features. For instance, we read under (c) that "the changes occur not fortuitously but according to certain laws" [27]; they are the "outcome of the accumulation of imperceptible and gradual quantitative changes" [28]; now these are ontological theses which have nothing to do with method. The same can be said of two fairly recent books by M. A. Leonov and M. M. Rozental', both called *The Marxist Dialectical Method;* they also do not deal with method but present Lenin's ontological theses. Lenin himself considered dialectic as the totality of laws of the 'objective world".[29] Secondly, it is evident that the theses put forward under the heading 'dialectic' are of secondary importance compared to those in the chapter on 'Materialism'. In this latter chapter Stalin gave a justification of realism which is, in his own words and teaching, the most fundamental doctrine of all.

Under the heading 'Materialism' he also dealt with *materiality*, i.e. the nature of reality. The spirit of the system makes it quite clear that these theses have precedence over those treated under 'Dialectic'. If the latter are placed first, this is due to the linguistic accident that in Russian the adjective precedes the noun.

Thirdly, the order in which the theses on materialism are presented is not satisfactory. For Lenin realism is of prime importance – and rightly so; and so it is difficult to understand why materiality is treated first. The more so, as the thesis of the materiality of being *(des Seins)* is an exceedingly complex and difficult problem in Dialectical Materialism. The problem involved in realism is much simpler.

And so we come to the conclusion that Stalin's 'classical' classification is useless. That is why we shall not follow it. We shall organize our study as follows: we begin with what Lenin calls 'materialism' – which covers his realism – i.e. thesis (b) in Stalin's analysis of 'materialism'. Logically connected with this thesis is the postulate that everything that is can be apprehended (c). Only then can we approach the problem of materiality (a). Having thus exhausted materialism, we shall move over to the dialectic and follow Stalin's classification. Finally, we shall briefly investigate the essential elements of Historical Materialism and its applications.

4. CONTENT OF THIS PHILOSOPHY: THE MISSING DISCIPLINES.
As we have pointed out, Dialectical Materialism includes the following:
1] An epistemology (extreme realism and rationalism).
2] A universally valid specific methodology, termed 'dialectical'.
3] A general system of metaphysics and ontology, which describes the characteristic features of all being *(des gesamten Seins)* (materialism, evolutionism, etc.); this metaphysics and ontology, being monistic and materialistic, coincides with cosmology.
As we shall see presently, Historical Materialism contains the following elements:

4] A social philosophy and a philosophy of history.

5] The foundations of a general and special axiology (theoretical ethics, aesthetics, philosophy of religion).

It is to be noted that in this system several disciplines are lacking which are considered classical disciplines in Western philosophy; for instance, formal logic, anthropology and ethics. Admittedly, they have an embryonic existence in the Soviet system but, unlike Dialectical and Historical Materialism which have a well-defined form, their position is very indefinite, thanks to Stalin. Logic, perhaps, enjoys the most favourable situation. Anthropology is represented only by psychology which, incidentally, is in a permanent state of crisis. Ethics is found in traces only; for the most part in pedagogy. These three disciplines give some insight into the dramatic struggle for intellectual liberty in those spheres where liberty of a kind is still permitted. We shall have more to say on this subject presently as well as on aesthetics – where the situation is similar.

5. THE SITUATION OF FORMAL LOGIC. Hegel identified logic with dialectic, i.e. with his own ontology, and rejected formal logic; on this particular point Dialectical Materialism has remained true to Hegel and for a long time there was no doctrine of logic in Soviet Russia. In November 1948, the Central Committee of the Party resolved to introduce it into the curriculum of secondary and advanced schools and of universities [30]; already in 1948, 140 professors of logic took part in a congress. [31] Also, lectures on logic were given at the Institute of Philosophy of the Academy of Sciences. [32] Because these lectures did not belong to the course on Dialectical and Historical Materialism, they are not compulsory for those who are to become teachers of the fundamental doctrine of the Party. Apparently Soviet logicians too worked along lines which were not approved by the authorities. For instance, the teaching of the professor of logic, P.S. Popov, was condemned, by a decree of the Minister for Higher Education, S. V. Kaftanov (March 23 1948), on the grounds of his formalism, scholasticism and lack of political consciousness (apoliti-čnost'). [33] Similar accusations were levelled at V. F. Asmus' book Logica a textbook of classical logic of a level similar to that of Western textbooks of around 1910 [34]. This book gave rise to a violent discussion among the

140 professors of logic mentioned above. The discussion was organized in June 1948, in Moscow, by the Ministry for Higher Education, the Academy of Social Science and the Institute of Philosophy. Asmus was found guilty of ideological insufficiency *(bezidejnost')* and of formalism while his logic was condemned for being apolitical. Osmakov reported that he even 'had the nerve to defend himself', but that he was supported by only a couple of those present. The others condemned his doctrine for being 'non-partisan and neutral' logic. [35] In fact, in July 1949, the Ministry for Higher Education issued a 'programme for logic' in which are to be found expressions like: 'partisanship of the science of logic'; 'Soviet logic – a sharp ideological weapon...'. [36] In other words, logic was only tolerated and had no easy existence.

The logicians were encouraged by Stalin's declaration that language is not a superstructure and therefore independent of class. In 1950–1951, i.e. immediately after Stalin's intervention, they organized a large-scale discussion in which 15 logicians and philosophers participated. In an editorial retrospect *Voprosy Filosofii* had this to say: "There are not two different types of formal logic, the old, metaphysical logic, and the new, dialectical one... There is only one formal logic, which is generally applicable to humanity; it is the collection (sic!) of elementary rules of thinking..." Every attempt to amalgamate this logic with dialectic was uncompromisingly rejected on the strength of the usual quotations from Engels, Lenin and – naturally – Stalin. [37]

But a reverse was experienced after Stalin's death and Aleksandrov's dismissal (see above, Chapter III, 8). A letter from Boguslavskij and Tavanec tells us that since 1954, when many textbooks on logic were condemned, the idea of finding such a textbook has been abandoned and that professors of logic have no longer been trained. [38] In 1955 the above-mentioned discussion was violently attacked in the *Kommunist* (by M.B. Mitin) [39] and in a lead-article in *Voprosy Filosofii*. [40] The defenders of independent formal logic are branded as 'nihilists' and 'popularizers'. The lead-article says *inter alia:* "It is quite clear that the struggle between opinions has now overstepped the boundaries of Marxism... We must really put an end to this erroneous tendency." [41]

The situation since then has remained somewhat ambiguous. Evidently the supporters of formal logic are obstinate and will not admit defeat. As late as November 25 1955 permission to print a collection of essays on logic [42], was granted. Among them was one which defended formal logic and reflected the spirit of the 1950–1951 discussion. [43] In 1955 there also appeared a new textbook of formal logic which met with the approval of the official critics [43]; this was quite an elementary study and the logic is 'classical' in the worst sense of the word. At the same time – and this must be stressed – investigations of a formal logical nature flourish in the field of mathematics, i.e. outside the sphere of philosophy. [44]

6. THE SITUATION OF PSYCHOLOGY. Although Communist philosophy likes to describe itself as 'humanistic', it ignores philosophic anthropology. Even psychology has no assured future in Soviet Russia. It has experienced four phases which parallel those of philosophy: 1] First there was the chaos of a multitude of different tendencies (1917–1924); during this period (1922) the Soviet psychologists 'resolved' to find in Dialectical Materialism a foundation for their science. 2] The second period (1924–1930) was one of varied experiments which all failed. Attempts were made to replace psychology by a 'reflexology' (Bekterev), by a 'reactology' (Kornilov) and by a 'theory of cultural evolution' (Vygodskij); all these were, to some extent, copies of Western models. 3] In 1930 began a period of intensive criticism of these theories which ended in the condemnation of the so-called 'pedologues'. These are the psychologists who sought to apply psychotechnical methods extensively to education. The psychotechnical institutes were abolished, by a decree of the Central Committee, on July 4 1936; so were the school posts for psychologists. 4] Since then renewed efforts have been made to work out a form of psychology which would be based on Dialectical Materialism. Psychology developed to such an extent that in 1939 Russia stood fifth in the world according to the number of publications on psychology. [45] These publications seemed to indicate that the position of psychology was changing. Even in 1939 there was no article on psychology in the *Short Philosophical Dictionary*[46], but the main work written by S. L. Rubinštejn and published in 1940 is called *Principles of General Psychology*. In 1947 the Central Committee of the Party introduced psychology (under that name) as a compulsory subject at advanced schools. [48] The Institute of Philosophy now runs a course on psychology. [49]

In spite of all this, the position of psychology remains insecure; it is not a compulsory subject in the courses on Dialectical Materialism and the Party directives, as to its content and lines to be followed, change constantly. For instance, Rubinštejn's book (1940) which considers both sides of Dialectical Materialism – with special emphasis on 'leaps' and on 'connection' – was recommended as a textbook; the author even received the Stalin prize in 1942. Since about 1949 (the centenary of I. P. Pavlov's birth) a radical change has taken place. At the 1950 plenary session of the psychological section of the Academy of Sciences [50], Rubinštejn was condemned as an 'idealist'; a 'Pavlovian' direction, i.e. a more purely materialistic one, was prescribed. What the actual significance of this is often remains vague. [51]

The situation of these two disciplines (logic and psychology) shows what difficulties beset dialectical materialists as soon as they try to develop something which has not been defined firmly by the 'classics'.

7. THE SITUATION OF AESTHETICS AND OF ETHICS. The position of these two disciplines differs from that of logic and psychology in that a basis for a theory of ethics and of aesthetics can be found in Historical Materialism. Indeed, the 'Programme' contains a short paragraph on aesthetics [52] and a special paragraph on 'Communist morality' – but the two disciplines experienced different fates. Owing to Maxim Gorky's * influence, aesthetics has always been considered a legitimate discipline. For instance, a long article on aesthetics [53] appeared in the 1940 *Short Philosophical Dictionary*, but there was none on ethics; the only reference to ethics was in a few sentences, quoted from Lenin, which expressed the crudest utilitarianism. Later, however, both disciplines experienced a certain turn for the better. In connection with various decrees by the Central Committee, which condemned all forms of deviations by the artists, a discussion on aesthetics was organized, in March 1948, by the Academy of Social Sciences. [54] M. M. Rozental' presented a report and formulated the latest decisions which we shall consider presently. [55] I. V. Kuznecov pointed out how unfavourable the situation of aesthetics was in Soviet Russia; there were no chairs of aesthetics, no lectures and no theoretical research was being carried out. [56] However, the introduction of such lectures is already under consideration and as, early as 1948, V. F.

* Pseudonym for Alexej Maksimovič Peškov (1868–1930).

Berestnev and P. S. Trofimov had published a project for a course of lectures on 'the principles of Marxist-Leninist aesthetics'.

It was pedagogy which was responsible for the introduction of ethics. There are neither chairs of ethics nor lectures on ethics at the universities. M. Kalinin's book on *Communist Education,* published in 1946 and reprinted in several editions, contained some data on normative morality. It is impossible to educate the young without appealing to something more than what Lenin formulated as social utilitarianism; and so Kalinin's book contains many principles of traditional natural morality. The fourth edition of the *Short Philosophical Dictionary* already contains a longish article entitled 'Morality and Ethics'.[57] Even so, the small number of publications on ethics is striking when compared to those on aesthetics or even on logic.

REFERENCES: [1] DM 141. [2] KFS[2] 170b. [3] KFS[4] 350a. [4] Pr 313a; 'Rozental' M. dial. Method 1954, 8. [5] KFS[4] 350a. [6] Pr 313a. [7] ib. [8] Žd 259b. [9] ib. [10] Miller 50. [11] No. 11, in Pravda, 26. Jan. 1931. German in Wetter 1952, 593 et seq. [12] DM 141. [13] BSE 22. 133, KFS[2] 292a. [14] Pr 313a. [15] On the part played, 472 (Sočinenija 18, 187). [16] DM 141. [17] ib. [18] DM 143. [19] ib. [20] DM 144. [21] DM 147. [22] DM 150. [23] DM 151. [24] DM 152, [25] Sviderskij 304. [26] Pr 313–337. [27] DM 144. [28] ib. [29] ME 375; MEM 278. [30] Tavanec-Boguslavskij 220. [31] Osmakov 376a. [32] Vasilev 369b. [33] Vyšinskij 344. 34. Vojšvillo; American review, by S. P. Maslov in: Journ. of Philos. 46.1949.105 et seq. [35] Osmakov 376b. [36] VF 1951.6.143. [37] AaO 144. [38] Tavanec-Boguslavskij. 221 [39] Mitin 1955. [40] *Protiv putanicy . . .* [41] *Ibid.* 171. [42] *Voprosy Logiki.* [43] E. K. Vojšvillo, *K Voprosu* 20 et seq. [44] Gorsky; book review, VF 1956, 3, 214 et seq. [45] Cf. on this point and on the whole question since 1946: Kline 1956. [45] Tomaševskij 12. [46] KFS[2]. [47] KFS[4]. [48] Tomaševskij 12. [49] Vasilev 369b. [50] *Naučnaja Sessija . . .* 1950. [51] On this whole question see I. London 1952. [52] Pr 326a. [53] KFS[2]. 323 et seq. [54] Soveščanie . . .; on 10.2 the opera '*Velikaja Družba*' was condemned, see Werth. [55] Rozental' 1948(2). [56] *Zadači* 288. [57] KFS[4] 366 et seq. [58] Šarija, Šiškin.

VI. REALISM AND RATIONALISM

1. THE PROBLEM. As Engels says [1], as Lenin quotes [2] and as Stalin repeats [3], "the highest problem of all philosophy is that of the relationship between thinking and being, between mind and nature." According to the answer which philosophers find for this question Engels calls them idealists or materialists.

This thesis can be interpreted in one of two ways. 1] First of all it is an epistemological problem if one sees in it predominantly the opposition between thinking and being. In this case the question is one of knowing whether thought calls forth being (idealism) or whether thought comprehends being which exists independently of thought (realism). A realist can be either a materialist or a spiritualist; for realism merely requires that being should be recognized as existing independently of thought and does not specify whether this being is in fact purely material or spiritual. 2] On the other hand this thesis can also lead one to ask the *cosmological* question, namely whether mind or nature (material nature) comes first; if one believes the former one is a spiritualist, if the latter one is a materialist. Apart from these, various other intermediate positions can be adopted.

For the Communists, whom we shall still have occasion to examine, the problem has yet a third meaning; it can be interpreted as a *Platonic problem*. But, to begin with, we shall treat the first two interpretations. Dialectical Materialism does not draw the distinction between 1] and 2] which Western philosophy draws; the dialectical materialists merely repeat Engels' thesis while attributing universal validity to it. This makes it considerably more difficult to understand their thought and is a source of great confusion in their doctrine.

We shall endeavour to elucidate the manifold elements of Communist materialism which, itself, is founded on an equivocal statement of the problem.

2. DEFINITION OF MATTER. We must return to Lenin if we want to understand this problem; for *he* did make a real contribution to this problem in Marxism, while his successors – apart from Markov to whom we shall return – contributed nothing that can be compared in originality to his doctrine. Lenin observed the disappearance of matter (in the classical sense of the word) in modern physics and introduced the differentiation between the physical and the philosophical conceptions of matter. By physical characteristics he means those which empirical science attributes to matter at any given moment.

This physical concept changes continually while the philosophical concept remains constant. Lenin's definition of matter in the philosophical sense runs as follows: "Matter is a philosophic category used for designating objective reality which man perceives with the aid of his senses, which our senses copy, photograph, reproduce and which exists apart from our senses..."[4] Also: "...the *only* 'property' of matter which materialism is absolutely bound to recognize is its property of *being objective reality*"[5]; furthermore: "the concept 'matter'... viewed from the epistemological point of view... means *one thing only*... it is objective reality, existing independently of human consciousness and reflected by it".[6] It is clear that the problem here is not one of the senses but of consciousness in general. The meaning of these passages, which are repeated by the Communists on every possible occasion, is quite unambiguous. Lenin's approach is the one described under 1] at the beginning of this chapter; his "materialism" is, above all, realistic and he affirms the primacy of *being* over *thinking*.

However, he immediately moves over to another conception of matter; having stated that the only property of matter, in the philosophic sense, is that it is independent of consciousness, he says, "Nothing exists in the world except matter in motion, and matter in motion cannot move except in time and space."[7] He also quotes Engels, whose thought he accepts: "Time and space are... conditions affecting the nature... of being *(des Seins)*."[8] Moreover, matter is perceived by the senses: it is therefore no longer simply what is *(das Seiende)* in general, but matter in the classical sense of the word. Here Lenin has abandoned the first for the second position from which to view the problem. Stalin followed his lead. Having defined realism in the paragraph quoted he continues with "...thought is a product of matter... to be precise a product of the brain"[9], even though he does devote a special paragraph to materialism itself. All other dialectical materialists proceed in like manner.

It was apparently due to historical considerations that Lenin gave his realism the name 'materialism'. In this he followed Engels who used this word in the same way.[10] Thus he could attack idealism of Berkeley who, in fact, did want to suppress matter.[11] Finally, Lenin had to deal with the *immanentists* of the *empiriocriticist* school who considered themselves realists although actually they were idealists.

Neither the ambiguity with which Engels formulated the problem, nor Lenin's slithering from one conception of matter to another, nor historical circumstances can alter anything in the fact that Dialectical Materialism today is strictly realistic. Its champions may confuse realism with materialism but they remain realists and very radical realists at that.

68

There are passages in Marx which can be interpreted in an idealistic manner; such an interpretation is impossible in the case of Lenin and his disciples.

3. JUSTIFICATION AND INTERPRETATION OF REALISM. This realism is usually accepted as an axiom and justified, by reference to principles, almost incidentally. In Lenin we find three types of demonstration. 1] The first and most frequent justification is based on the affirmation that science has demonstrated the existence of the universe long before the existence of consciousness. [12] 2] In his second demonstration, Lenin based himself on practical life and quoted Engels' statement: "This is the fundamental error in idealism, namely, that it poses to itself and solves the problem of objectivity and subjectivity, of the reality or unreality of the world, only from the theoretical point of view".[13] "For in human existence practice is important not only as a phenomenon in Hume's and Kant's interpretation of the word, but has also objectively real significance".[14] After quoting Engels' famous dictum, "The proof of the pudding is in the eating", he adds, "Objects exist outside of ourselves. Our perceptions and notions are images of them. In actual practice these images are submitted to a test which separates the correct from the incorrect ones".[15] 3] Finally, the following demonstration is often found in Lenin: idealism leads to the recognition of the existence of God; but there is no God; therefore idealism is fallacious. All these proofs are very weak; the last one quite remarkably so, for it is a well-known fact that epistemological idealism excludes the recognition of God's existence. But neither Lenin nor his disciples attach much importance to proving their theses. We cannot but observe that it is here much more a matter of faith than of a doctrine to be proved.

A detailed analysis of realism is only possible after a description of Dialectical and Historical Materialism, for the epistemology of Dialectical Materialism is a complex matter. That is why we begin by describing what this type of realism understands by knowledge. In this connection the most fundamental statement is that the object is "copied, photographed, reproduced" by our consciousness. [16] Lenin comes back again and again to the following idea: materialism is a theory of 'reflection' *(otraženija)*, our perceptions are images of reality [17], consciousness forms a reflected image of the laws of the universe [18], materialism deals with our images [19], it sees in our consciousness an image of reality. [20] That is why the Communists replace the term 'epistemology' by the term 'theory of reflection' *(teorija otraženija)*. [21]

When it comes to analyzing how we can apprehend reality Lenin adopts the attitude of an illationist realism: "The various sensations of colour can be explained by reference to the different wave lengths of light which exist outside of the human retina, outside man and independently of him... This is just what materialism is: matter acts on our sense organs and creates sensation." [22] Naturally there arises here the following difficulty: how can the sensation of a colour be the reflected image of a light wave? Dialectical materialists today reply to this objection by saying that 'the objective colour quality of the light wave is reflected in the subjective form, in sensation. Colour is something resembling the activity of light." [23] The least that can be said of this explanation is that it is incapable of explaining anything.

Whatever else they have to say on this subject does not belong to the theory of knowledge but to the sphere of psychology; indeed, they attempt to give a more accurate description of the psychological process of apprehending knowledge without bothering about its nature. An exception is represented by Markov's noteworthy essay.

4. MICROPHYSICAL COGNITION ACCORDING TO MARKOV. Latterly we find in Soviet philosophical publications attempts to give an explanation of the nature of knowledge; not, however, of knowledge in general, but of knowledge in the microphysical sphere. This has been the most noteworthy work in Soviet philosophy for a long time and deserves detailed study even though, after a bitter struggle, it has been condemned. It appears in M. A. Markov's *On the Nature of Physical Cognition (Erkenntnis)* published in 1947.

Although it could have been otherwise, man is a macrophysical being, and only macrophysical phenomena are accessible to his senses. It follows that if the microphysical world is to be apprehended by man this can take place only by means of a 'transference' with the aid of macrophysical instruments, of the phenomena and laws of the microphysical world, into a macrophysical 'language'. This is in fact what happens; what we know are the macrophysical records made by our instruments. Two conclusions can be drawn from this: *a)* the action of the instrument, i.e.

of man, must penetrate into the structure of the microphysical world. Therefore the question "what does the electron as such, without reference to the observer, look like?" is as senseless as the question "what is the path of a movement as such, without reference to any coordinates?" *b*) The transference is never unequivocal: it depends on the instruments which are used, in other words on the nature of man's activity.

This does not lead to idealism. For, even though human activity is drawn into the microphysical object, the fact remains that we have here a real form of activity, an actually existing relationship between a real subject and a no less real object. If the physicist is unable to perceive simultaneously the mechanical impulse and the position of the particle, nevertheless he knows perfectly well when there *is* a particle and when there is not; he can therefore say a good deal about microphysical reality.

But it is important to avoid two errors: first of all, metaphysical materialism, which fails completely to take human activity into account and which, so to speak, submerges completely in the object because it forgets that knowledge is the result of a relationship between subject and object; the other source of error is idealism which concerns itself only with the subjective aspect of cognition and overlooks the fact that cognition requires a *real* object and that it is itself a *real* activity. Only Dialectical Materialism, which recognizes simultaneously the objectivity of cognition and the part played in it by human activity, can give microphysics a firm base. In doing this, Dialectical Materialism does not, by any means, step beyond its proper sphere; for, even when dealing with man's knowledge of the macrophysical universe it stresses the importance of human activity as an integral element of all epistemological activity.

5. PERCEPTIBILITY OF THE WORLD. *Radical rationalism* is intimately linked with Leninist realism. Here too, according to Stalin [24], the enemy is idealism; but, according to Lenin the enemy is twofold; agnosticism which says that the true being of the world cannot be comprehended, and 'fideism', which "gives faith primacy over science". This subject, which Stalin treats under heading (c) of 'materialism', is dealt with in a long paragraph in the 'Programme' under the heading "Perceptibility of the World and of its Laws" *(zakonomernosti)*. [25] Three theses are put forward: 1] the world and its laws are entirely perceptible [26]; 2] "our scientific knowledge of the laws governing nature" is "reliable knowledge"... the

laws of nature represent "objective truth"[27]; 3] things which are not yet known will be discovered and comprehended with the aid of science.[28]

1] The *perceptibility of reality* is stressed in opposition to Kant. In a famous passage, Engels [29] once declared that industry had disproved the whimsical notion that the 'thing in itself' could not be perceived; by producing alizarine, chemistry had transformed the 'thing in itself' into a 'thing for us'; the same effect was achieved by Leverrier's and Galle's discovery of a new planet. Lenin adopted this passage of Engels [30] and Stalin repeated it [31]; the 'Programme' devoted a paragraph to it. [32] Lenin even attempted to justify this strange demonstration against V. M. Černov who in 1907 had subjected it to a thoroughly justified criticism. Lenin accused him of having substituted the 'not perceived' for the 'not perceptible', for the 'thing in itself' [33]; he thus held that the case of alizarine proved objects and bodies exist externally to, and independently of, us and that there is no distinction between the 'thing in itself' and 'the thing for us'; and lastly, he says that we can ascertain a 'dialectical' transition from ignorance to knowledge. [34] Obviously this argumentation in no manner justifies Engels' untenable procedure. But it serves to emphasize the fact that we need not look for proofs in these authors; they merely state their beliefs.

2] When attacking the 'empiriocriticists' Lenin had stressed with great energy the fact that objective, *absolute truth* exists and is perceptible [35]; for Stalin our perception has the 'significance' of an absolute truth.[36] According to the 'Programme' [37] this is founded on the theory of reflection. Now, apart from absolute truth there also exist relative truths; the former 'derives' from the latter [38] and in such a manner "that there is no unbridgeable gulf between relative and absolute truth in Dialectical Materialism".[39] Lenin on the other hand said that absolute truth is "composed of the sum of relative truths as they develop" [40]; all of which is rather obscure. In the *Philosophical Notebooks* we find a passage which expresses Lenin's idea rather better; "knowledge *(die Erkenntnis)* is an eternal, unceasing approach of thought towards its object. The reflection of nature in human thought must not be conceived in a lifeless, abstract, stationary manner." [41]

Connected with the problem of objective truth is that of reality *(das Wesen)*. According to the dialectic there can be no unchanging reality. [42] But *there are* realities: "it is reality that reveals itself; the appearance is something real". [43] The process itself is reality. [44] This reality is perceptible. This doctrine, developed by M. Mitin [45], has been recently re-interpreted by M. Rozental' [46] as meaning that reality appears only in the *mass* of phenomena and not in an isolated phenomenon. In this, therefore, present-day Dialectical Materialism is strongly Aristotelian.

To this must be added (as we have said already) the belief that the criterion of our knowledge is to be found in practice. [47] But this part of the doctrine of Dialectical Materialism cannot yet be identified with pragmatism: practice is merely a criterion for reality; in fact one paragraph of the 'Programme' is devoted specifically to criticism of bourgeois pragmatism [48]; there James and Dewey are treated as idealists. [49] In this doctrine, therefore, a new assertion is added to the realistic thesis: our consciousness is not only a 'copy' of reality, but an 'objective copy' – and there is no reality that is not perceptible.

3] This is not the place to dwell on scientific *optimism* which believes that science will discover everything; which is only a repetition of the familiar ideas of eighteenth and nineteenth century materialists.

6. THE IDEOLOGICAL FOUNDATIONS OF THE DOCTRINES. Our treating rationalism and realism together was intentional, for both doctrines seem to occupy a similar position within the framework of Lenin's conception of the world. As is the case with most tenets of present-day Dialectical Materialism, we have here not so much philosophical theses, which rest upon experience and analysis, as expressions of a deep faith, which is defended with the energy characteristic of faith. This is not the place to submit the justification of these tenets of faith to criticism; whoever is familiar with the problems which are mentioned here will observe without difficulty that none of the 'proofs' which Dialectical Materialism utilizes really deserves that name. The reasons which made Lenin and his successors accept these doctrines were not the ones which they cite.

One of the reasons can be seen in Lenin's character: he viewed the world from the standpoint of an engineer, of a technician; he considered the world, humanity and the individual as raw material, which was to be fashioned technically, or as a site, which he was called upon to exploit. Such a perspective naturally presupposes both realism and radical rationalism. Lenin is a realist because, as a man of action, he cannot admit that the world, which he works and transforms, can be anything but real; he is a realist also because that is the natural and inevitable attitude for a man of action to adopt, whatever the idealists may have to say about it. Rationalism, too, is a concomitant of such a character: concerned with the transformation of the world by technical means, Lenin cannot admit that factors which cannot be comprehended exist in this world, for such factors would be inaccessible to the conscious activity of a man of action.

There is something else which, apparently, is even more important. Lenin's conception of the world is pivoted round his hatred of religion; and he thought that idealism, agnosticism and 'fideism' inevitably lead to religion. Admittedly idealism is inherently hostile to transcendental religion, but the situation in the case of agnosticism and 'fideism' is not as straightforward as Lenin thought. But this does not alter the fact that he believed in a connection between these doctrines and religion. And religion he will not have at any price. This is the basic reason why he rejected idealism and insisted on the absolute perceptibility of the world. In all this the dialectical materialists of today have remained faithful to Lenin; they have retained his doctrines, nay even his errors, down to the reasoning which he used against Kant and which strikes us as monstrous.

REFERENCES: [1] LF 28(27). [2] ME 85. [3] DM 151. [4] ME 117; KFS[2] 161a. [5] ME 261. [6] ME 262. [7] ME 167; KFS 161a; Pr. 319a. [8] ME 167; KSF 34b. [9] DM 151. [10] ME 41. [11] ME 7. [12] ME 59 et seq. [13] ME 130. [14] ME 92. [15] ME 96; Pr 39b. [16] ME 117; KFS 161a. [17] 94. [18] ME 162. [19] ME 267. [20] ME 268. [21] Dosev; KFS[2] 277 et seq; [4]597b et seq. [22] ME 37. [23] Mitin 1933, 120. [24] DM 152. [25] Pr 319a. [26] DM 152. [27] DM 153 et seq. [28] DM 153. [29] LF 29 et seq. [30] ME 86. [31] DM 153. [32] Pr 319b. [33] ME 87. [34] ME 89. [35] ME 120. [36] DM 152. [37] Pr 319b. [38] ME 122. [39] ME 123. [40] ME 314; Pr 319b. [41] FT 168; Pr 319b. [42] ME 263; KFS 161a. [43] KFS 270a; Pr 319 et seq. [44] FT 174. [45] Mitin 1933, 175. [46] Rozental' 1947, 327 et seq. [47] FT 164. [48] Pr 313b. [49] KFS 217; Šostin; Gagarin.

VII. MATERIALISM

I. MULTIPLE MEANING OF THE WORD. We have seen that Dialectical Materialism states the fundamental problem of philosophy in an ambiguous fashion: this problem can be interpreted either as an epistemological or as an ontological one. Even if it is interpreted in this latter sense, 'materialism' in Communist philosophy is anything but a homogeneous doctrine: it is composed of a complex of statements some of which only partly depend one on the other while others are not only independent of one another but belong to quite different fields of investigation. These statements can be classed in three main groups: metaphysical, ontological and psychological.

1] The first group of these materialist theses considers the *existence* of certain real beings; here Bolshevik theory is first and foremost anti-theological, it denies the existence of God. 2] In the second group are to be found ontological doctrines, using the word 'ontological' as Husserl used it; they deal with the *essence* of reality in general. Here also we come across two problems and two doctrines which the Communists always confuse but which are undoubtedly contained in their doctrine. These are: the belief that all reality is by its very nature exclusively material and, on the other hand, the denial of ideal being *(eines idealen Seins)* in the Platonic sense. 3] The third group contains those theses of Dialectical Materialism which deal with the *relations between mind and matter,* i.e. theses of a psychological nature. It is doubtful, of course, whether such questions can be asked at all once the existence of any spiritual element in reality has been denied. But we shall see that, in fact, the Communists do put forward these two problems at different levels.

Some of the theses mentioned above are not connected one with the other, with the result that the Communists oppose to their materialism not only deism, spiritualism or Platonism but also psychological doctrines such as speculative parallelism. They do so because they consider all these doctrines to be but one single philosophy and use only *one* term to express the contrast between them and the various aspects of materialism: this word is 'idealism' which, incidentally, they also use in their epistemology. In their opinion, everyone is an idealist who does not subscribe *in toto* to 'materialism'. We shall now examine in detail what is understood by this 'materialism'.

2. METAPHYSICAL THESES. Four theses can be distinguished: 1] The first derives from Heraclitus' dictum that "none of the gods has created the world nor has man" which Lenin called "an excellent formulation of the principles of Dialectical Materialism".[1] This means that the

75

world was not created. 2] Furthermore, the world is eternal [2]; or rather, nothing is eternal except matter and the laws of motion; also, the world is infinite in space. [3] Let it be observed that this thesis is quite independent of the first one: for instance, St. Thomas Aquinas teaches that the creation of the world by God can be proved but that its creation in time *sola fide tenetur*. According to Heraclitus, the world develops exclusively in obedience to the laws of matter in motion; this development does not require a "spirit of the universe" [4]; in other words: the universe is autonomous not only with regard to the origin of its existence but also with regard to the continuance of this existence: God is not required, either as creator or as maintainer. 4] It follows that the "material world which can be perceived by the senses and to which we ourselves belong is the only true reality" [5]; this is the real monistic thesis which states that nothing exists outside of the world.

No attempt is made in Soviet philosophical literature to prove these theses; they are in fact, of course, not theses which could be proved but beliefs which Lenin and Engels took over from the 'vulgar' materialists of the nineteenth century: in this context Lenin's enthusiasm for Haeckel [6] is very revealing. The main argument that is constantly brought up in order to disprove the existence of God is that movement is an essential property of matter. [7]

3. ONTOLOGICAL THESES. A second group of theses concerns itself with the substance of actual things. Here four viewpoints can be distinguished in Stalin's argument: 1] The world is not the embodiment of an absolute idea. [8] Although this statement is aimed immediately at Hegel, what Stalin really expresses in it is radical anti-Platonism which denies the existence of any ideal element preceding the existence of the real world. As the existence of God is denied, there can be no question of divine ideas acting as models for the world; but it would still have been possible to conceive a world of ideas in Plato's sense. The dialectical materialists confuse these pure ideas with the subjective (psychic) ideas in our consciousness; but their contempt of Plato is ample proof of the fact that their main concern is to reject Platonism, whether or not they confuse the ideal and the spiritual in the process. 2] Also, "the world is material in its nature". [9] We shall presently examine in greater detail the word "material"; but one thing is clear already: Stalin wants to reject

not only Platonism but also any system which conceives the nature of the universe to be, perhaps, 'vital', as in Bergson's *élan vital* or 'spiritual' as with Hegel. This also means that the 'nature' of the world has but one single basic form, the material one; there are not several different basic forms of *being*; in other words, this is a monistic conception of nature. 3] Matter is the subject of any change that takes place.[10] This 'subject' is evidently a notion similar to the 'substance' of Scholasticism; even though Lenin rejects the word 'substance', nevertheless Deborin is perfectly right in saying: "In the system of materialistic logic the main concept must be that of matter as substance".[11] The substance behind all changes is material. 4] Finally: "The manifold phenomena in the world represent various forms of matter in motion".[12] While defining the preceding theses more accurately – phenomena here seem to be a conception similar to that of the *accidentia* of Scholasticism – this fourth thesis also introduces a new element: matter *in motion* is what makes up reality. We shall examine the nature of movement when we come to speak of dialectic. This is a sequence of ontological theses: the first one occupies a special position and expresses anti-Platonic feelings; the other three define rather more exactly what materialism means ontologically. Obviously their meaning depends on the meaning that is given to the word 'matter'.

4. PROPERTIES OF MATTER. We have already said that Lenin draws a distinction between matter in the philosophical and matter in the physical sense. Now which particular type of matter do the above-mentioned theses refer to? Evidently, not to matter in the physical sense for this is a relative, variable notion which depends on the state of science at any given moment, while in these theses matter is spoken of as being a fundamental notion whose validity does not depend on the evolution of science. Matter in the philosophical sense is determined by its essential properties: movement, space, time.
The word 'movement' *(dviženie)* is interpreted in its widest sense as 'becoming', 'developing'. "The principal forms of movement are: mechanical..., physical..., chemical..., intra-atomic movement..., organic development..., i.e. life..., life in society..., consciousness."[13] In other words: "The notion 'movement' includes every type of change: change of quality, of form, of composition and change in the relationship

with environment".[14] Movement, thus defined, is conceived as an inherent property of matter and as the normal form of existence for matter. [15] It would, therefore, seem clear that for the dialectical materialists this conception of movement does not define the word 'matter' as something material in the usual sense of the word: if it is said that movement is the essential property of matter, this means that everything that is – is in process of becoming – and no more than that.

The situation changes, of course, if we take time and space into account. Indeed, according to Engels, movement is "the combination of time and space". It is, therefore, not surprising to read in Lenin: "Nothing exists in the world apart from matter in motion, and matter cannot move except in time and space"[16]; and later on: "The basic forms of all existence are space and time"[17]; they are forms "which are most intimately and inevitably linked to matter".[18] Therefore, every movement, i.e. all development, is movement *in space*. This whole doctrine, therefore, borrows its essential characteristics not only from classical but also from mechanistic materialism, although its supporters deny any connection with it.

Another property of matter is that it is infinite, not only in space and in time but also in 'depth' [19]: this means, it would seem, that it is infinitely divisible. "Nature in its sum as well as in its parts has no beginning and no end", Lenin repeated after Dietzgen.[20]

What is particularly striking in this doctrine – apart from its materialism – is its deeply substantialist character. Movement without matter is inconceivable [21]; space and time are inconceivable without matter [22]; and, as we have seen, matter is the substratum of all changes which are its 'manifestations'. Also, only matter and its laws are eternal while everything else is changing constantly.[23]

Now if this is so, then it would be conceivable that while the substance was material – in the classical as well as in the current sense – its various forms, its manifestations, should belong to different stages of being. The statement that the *substance* of the world is material does not necessarily imply categorial monism or categorial pluralism. It would be possible for the phenomena of such matter not to be material. At any rate there arises here the problem of the relations between the different stages of its manifestations. These problems are dealt with in the third group of materialist theses, those which are concerned with psychology.

5. PSYCHOLOGICAL THESES. Here, too, four different theses can be distinguished: 1] "Thought cannot be separated from matter..." [24] Thought without a brain is an absurdity, says Lenin. This thesis which leads people to deny the substantiality of the spirit and consequently the immortality of the soul is not necessarily materialistic. 2] But the following statements are. "The spirit or mind is of secondary importance" [25] and "consciousness is only... the image of matter". [26] Doubtless this is first and foremost an epistemological statement; but the fact that here Lenin speaks of the spirit or mind in general shows that this is partly a psychological thesis. Mind is, in a manner of speaking, a concomitant of certain material processes and subordinate to them because it is called forth by them. Incidentally, Lenin deduces from this the basic thesis of Historical Materialism according to which "social consciousness reflects social reality". [27] 3] "Matter thinks" [28] – means that thought is a *function* of matter. Now, most classical texts say "thought is a product of the brain and the brain is the organ of thinking". [29] "Thought is the product of matter organized in a specific way". [30]
It is very difficult to grasp the exact meaning of these theses, especially if one takes into account what dialectic says on this matter. It is not clear just what kind of materialism the Communists represent; for there are several mutually exclusive forms of it. If mind is a concomitant, it is not a product of matter; and if it is one or the other, it cannot be a function. On the other hand dialectic teaches that there is a 'leap' *(skačok)* between crude matter and life, between life and consciousness; therefore, the material 'substance' from which issue all these functions must be something after all which is neither crude matter nor life nor mind. If it were not for dialectic this problem would be easier for the dialectical materialists to solve – and this thesis still remains an impenetrable mystery in the system.

6. LENIN AND SCIENTIFIC MATERIALISM. From what has just been said we can conclude that Dialectical Materialism today repeats the essential doctrines of so-called "classical", i.e. scientific materialism. There is, however, more than just this to be found in Lenin; he specifically professed belief in these doctrines. Indeed, in a discussion with Bogdanov, Lenin said that Engels criticized 'Büchner & Co' for three reasons only: because they conceived materialism in an exclusively mechanistic

way, because they remained 'anti-dialectical' and because they retained idealism in the field of social sciences.[31] Lenin added: "Engels rejects eighteenth century materialism *exclusively* for these three reasons and *exclusively* within these limits! In all other problems, which belong more to the ABC of materialism and which were distorted by the followers of Mach, *there is no difference and there can be no difference* between Marx and Engels on the one hand and all these old materialists on the other."[32] Here, as always, Lenin accepted Engels' claims.

Now, we have not come across one single text in Soviet Russian philosophic literature which rejected this doctrine of Lenin; and, after what we have said about the spirit of this literature and about Lenin's position as a 'classic', it is clear that there can be no such text. Dialectical Materialism has other components as well, but everything that characterizes classical materialism also belongs to Dialectical Materialism. This fact must be particularly emphasized because, for purposes of propaganda, it is often denied in the West and a 'dialectical' and therefore 'mitigated' form of materialism is attributed to Communism. In actual fact, their materialism is by no means 'mitigated'; it is, on the contrary, pure, classical materialism.

7. JUSTIFICATION OF MATERIALISM: ITS POSITION IN THE COMMUNIST CONCEPTION OF THE WORLD. Proof of these materialistic theses is very summary and is mostly based on the results of scientific research in a manner reminiscent of nineteenth century materialistic literature. No proof is adduced for the anti-Platonic and substantialist doctrines. As for the others, they are not so much proved theorems as expressions of a faith which, together with their demonstration, are drawn from classical materialism. At this juncture we refer the reader once more to Lenin's enthusiasm for Haeckel.[33] Incidentally, everything that has been said about realism and rationalism applies also in this connection to the Communist doctrine.

The first thing to strike the reader, especially in the metaphysical theses of this materialism, is the atheism which, for Lenin, was of decisive importance. Here, in a way, can be found the source of his thought. His atheism, which, as we know, was also due to the influence of Russian revolutionary thought, becomes more comprehensible when we consider the basic features of his character as we have done already. Lenin was primarily an engineer, a technician and a man of action. As an engineer whose ambition was to transform the world, he needed three things above all others: he must be alone in the world, unhampered by any competition; God would be a dangerous competitor, and so the mere idea that he might exist could not be tolerated. Furthermore, the world must be in every way capable of being fashioned just as a material is capable of being fashioned by a technician; the world must, therefore, be material and suitable for technical manipulation. Finally, Lenin wanted to manipulate not only the world, but also men; therefore humanity, too, must in a sense be similar to matter and obey the general laws which govern matter; here is the origin of psychological materialism. Here the ultimate foundations of materialism, in the narrower sense of the word, meet those of realism and of rationalism. All three of these doctrines are based, in a similar fashion, on the activist and technical attitude of Lenin and his disciples.

When one views the situation from this angle a certain unity becomes apparent among the various meanings of the word 'idealism' which are often mutually so contradictory; also the reason becomes obvious why this 'idealism' is so violently rejected by the Communists. As we have seen, the latter call an idealist anyone, 1] who claims that consciousness engenders being; 2] who admits the existence in reality of factors which cannot be perceived; 3] who believes in God; 4] who admits the existence of ideal factors in Plato's sense; 5] who teaches that reality contains something else besides matter; 6] who claims for the mind independence from the body.

As has already been said, some of these doctrines have no connection one with the other; for instance, the Thomists agree with the dialectical materialists in rejecting theses 1], 2] and 4] and, partly, thesis 6], but believe that theses 3] and 5] are correct; similar examples could be provided by contrasting Dialectical Materialism with other contemporary Western philosophies.

A twofold bond which unites these six theses is expressed in Lenin's above-mentioned attitude and in the historical origin of these doctrines; for, as we have seen, they can all be traced back to the eighteenth and nineteenth century materialists. Admittedly some of these theses have taken a bias, in this or that direction, as a result of Lenin's Russian origin, but it is also true that Lenin himself made every effort to lead materialism out of its classical stage, in which matter was viewed as the sum total of mechanically moving atoms, and to give it a more general form. But his efforts have failed, and the materialist substance contained in Dialectical Materialism is fundamentally the same as that of classical materialism.

Meanwhile this materialism is given a specific character by the other essential element of Communist philosophy: its dialectic.

REFERENCES: [1] FT 338; DM 150 et seq. [2] Ib.; KF 160b. [3] KFS 160b; BSE 22, 130. [4] DM 150. [5] DM 151. [6] ME 355 et seq.; KFS 40b. [7] AD 49; ME 257; Mitin 1934, 111. [8] DM 150. [9] ib. [10] DM 152. [11] *Gegel i dialektičeskij materializm* (Hegel's works in Russian, L, 1929), S. XC. quot. after Wetter 1948, 259. [12] DM 150. [13] KFS 54b. [14] Volfson-Gak 39; Pr 316b. [15] KFS 54a; Pr 316b. [16] ME 167. [17] AD 41; ME 169. [18] KFS 34b; BSE 22, 130; Pr 319a. [19] FT 112. [20] ME 262. [21] ME 267 et seq. [22] ME 167 et seq. [23] KFS 160b; see also Chapter 8. [24] DM 152. [25] ME 136; DM 151. [26] ME 329; DM 152. [27] ME (1951) 314. [28] ME 363; DM 152. [29] DM 151, cf ME 71 et seq. [30] KFS 178b; Pr 318b. [31] ME 238 et seq.; Harper, p. 88, summarizes this incorrectly. [32] ME 239. [33] ME 355 et seq.

VIII. THE DIALECTIC

1. MEANING OF THE WORD. CLASSIFICATION. In philosophic writings the word 'dialectic' has four distinct meanings. First of all it refers to the art of discussion and, in Plato, to metaphysics as well; thus it acquires the meaning 'logic', logic of probability (with Aristotle) and logic in general (in the Renaissance); for Kant the word represents the sum of natural and nevertheless fallacious deductions; finally, Hegel defines dialectic as follows: it is "the very nature of thinking"[1]; as, however, with Hegel, the laws of thinking and of being coincide, dialectic is for him "the specific and true nature of rational definitions, of things and of the finite in general".[2] In other words, Hegel sees in dialectic the totality of laws which determine the evolution of *being*. Judin and Rozental' agree with Hegel when they declare: "The dialectic is the science of the general laws of evolution in nature, in human society and in thought."[3] This dialectic plays an exceedingly significant part in Dialectical Materialism; Stalin calls it the "soul of Marxism".[4] Lenin, when he grew older, summoned the Soviet philosophers to study Hegel's dialectic with zeal.

In his opinion the editors of the periodical *Under the banner of Marxism* were to form "a kind of society of materialistic friends of Hegel's dialectic" [5]; he himself gave a lead by his studies in this field which find expression in his works.

According to Engels this dialectic comprises three laws: "The law of transition from quantity to quality and vice versa; the law of mutual interpenetration by the opposites and the law of negation of the negation." [6] Lenin distinguished in it no fewer than 16 essential points. [7] Stalin simplified Lenin's presentation and treated dialectic in 4 chapters where the essential theses are the following: 1] All phenomena are inter-related, 2] they are all involved in evolution; 3] this evolution progresses in dialectical 'leaps'; 4] the motive power is provided by the 'struggle' of the opposites.

Apart from the above-mentioned classification of dialectic we must also distinguish, as is now commonly done, between 'objective' and 'subjective' dialectic. 'Objective' dialectic investigates the laws of nature; 'subjective' dialectic deals with the laws of thinking and is therefore a kind of methodology and logic. We shall be following the current approach (admittedly not Stalin's) if we deal with these two aspects of dialectic separately.

Finally, we must draw attention to yet another distinction which is encountered in the writings of dialectical materialists today. They speak of the "fundamental features" *(osnovnye čerty)* and of the 'categories' of dialectic. The latter are "basic concepts of logic which reflect the most general and essential *(suščestvennye)* associations and connections of reality" [8]; as examples they name causality, necessity, content, form, etc. In spite of their universality they are considered to have evolved out of the 'general line' of dialectic. In the course of our investigation we shall step aside to examine briefly the most important of these categories.

2. THE GENERAL INTER-CONNECTION BETWEEN PHENOMENA. Stalin writes: "In contrast to metaphysics, dialectics sees in nature not a casual conglomeration of things and appearances unconnected one with the other, isolated from one another and independent of one another, but a well-knit homogeneous whole in which things and appearances are organically linked together, in which they depend on and influence one another." [9] In other words, there are no isolated phenomena; each phe-

nomenon belongs, at any given moment, to a whole with which it is organically associated. It is really surprising that this particular thesis is described as offering a contrast to metaphysics, for metaphysics has failed, if at all, by putting too much stress on this association rather than too little. This is just one more typical illustration of the rigidity of the Communists' view of history; this was how Hegel and Engels [10] viewed metaphysics, therefore these ideas must be repeated by the dialectical materialists. The doctrine itself stems from Hegel and was, as is well known, developed in detail by the English Hegelians. We are here referring to the claim that the connections of an individual with other individuals and with the whole constitute the substance of the individual, so that there is *nothing* in him apart from these connections. That is why Hegel can say: "the real" (i.e. the truly real) "is the whole" [11] and why he can consider the individual as just an 'instance' of this whole. This kind of analysis will not be found in the dialectical materialists; the nearest approach can be found in Lenin when he borrows the following statement from Hegel's *Enzyklopädie* (par. 216) and fits it into a context: "The individual members of the body are what they are only in their association with the body. The hand which has been separated from the body is a hand only in name!" [12] But the dialectical materialists teach that the unity of the world consists exclusively 'in its materiality'. [13]

That this is the central thesis of Communism can be seen from its social doctrine, its ethics and the practical application of the latter; for there the individual is considered as just such an "instance" without any true reality of his own. The first thesis of the dialectic therefore means much more than just an external, perhaps causal, connection between things. It is a very superficial formulation of an idea which is, perhaps, the ultimate foundation of Communist thought and conduct – although the Communists themselves have never fully clarified it. In this connection Stalin is particularly superficial; he cannot even draw the conclusion "therefore individualism and anarchism are fallacious".

This thesis is treated by the 1948 Programme together with the problem of causality *(pričinnost')*. Of course we do not find here a definition of causality or an attempt to prove the law of causality; but three theses are expressed with all necessary clarity: 1] Causality is objective in nature. Lenin had violently attacked Mach's conception that there was no causality in the world. [14] 2] This causality "is only a small part of the general inter-association of things, of the real, objective bond".[15] 3] Causality is always accompanied by a reaction and must be regarded as one element of a general reciprocal action.[16]

Connected with this is the problem of finality. According to Mitin the following is essential for the classical doctrine: there is no finality of any kind in nature; here can be found the reason for the dialectical materialists' enthusiasm for Darwinism. But we do find finality in human life, especially in the life of society.[17] One of Lenin's most important statements is the one which says that the process of nature *(stixijnost')* is not enough to bring about revolution; the doctrine of social determinism *(samotek =* 'self-flow') was condemned.

Revolution, as well as all evolution in society, requires a conscious activity and a conscious striving by man *(soznatel'nost')*[18] towards a goal. In the human sphere, therefore, there is finality. But it is only a form of causality; namely the form which causality assumes when nature 'leaps' into the human phase.

3. NECESSITY, CHANCE AND FREEDOM. Necessity is defined as the "objective obedience to laws *(zakonomernosti)* by phenomena"[19]: but Stalin taught that *all* changes occur "not fortuitously, but in obedience to certain laws"[20]: in other words, Dialectical Materialism is a strictly determinist doctrine even if it does not make use of the term. At any rate, indeterminism is rudely rejected.[21] Admittedly this determinism is 'dialectical', not 'mechanical', for it acknowledges the existence of chance *(slučajnost')* as an objective element of reality. Now, if the phenomena are strictly determined, what is understood by 'chance'? Two answers are given to this question. First of all, that is casual which occurs independently of the *inner* laws of existence applicable to the phenomenon; for instance, while growth of a plant is inevitable and firmly determined, its destruction by hail is casual.[22] Judging by this answer the emergence of effects from necessary causes would be fortuitous. There is also a second, a 'deeper explanation': the fortuitous is the relatively rare, that which occurs at irregular intervals; for instance, wages in the feudal age were fortuitous while in the capitalistic social order they have become a necessity obeying certain laws. Understood in this way, chance is a form of necessity, 'dialectically' linked to it.[23]

The doctrine of freedom is similar, though more complex. It can be summarized in two sentences of Engels. Engels writes: 1] "Freedom does not consist in the longed-for independence from the laws of nature, but in the knowledge of these laws and in the possibility arising therefrom of making them obey a plan and work towards definite goals". [24] Thus man, whose life is determined by laws which govern his existence, is called free if he is able to govern external nature. 2] "Only when man will be fashioning his history..., will there be a 'leap' out of the sphere of necessity into the sphere of freedom". [25] Here we are faced with one of Marx's fundamental ideas: in the capitalist system of society, economic life and, consequently, the whole life of man, stands under the rule of laws which operate independently of him, under the rule of "fetishism". Freedom, i.e. independence from these laws, can be assured by the Communist system alone; a social system in which the economy is consciously directed.

These lines of thought lead one to speak of 'Marxist humanism'; it is evident that all this has nothing to do with free will because the existence of the latter is simply denied in Dialectical Materialism.

We should like to take this opportunity to speak of the 'categories' of reality and of possibility. Reality must not be confused with existence; only that is real which is historically necessary, and vice versa. [26] Here, just as in their treatment of chance and of freedom, the dialectical materialists reject fatalism – which excludes conscious activity *(soznatel-nost')*. A distinction is drawn between abstract possibility (which belongs to all that which can be conceived by mind) and real possibility, which consists of the sum of the conditions which exist in reality. [27] From this Leonov drew the (paradoxical) conclusion that formal possibility was indistinguishable from impossibility since it is unrealizable; but this is not the generally accepted doctrine.

4. THE DOCTRINE OF EVOLUTION. "In contrast to metaphysics," says Stalin, "the dialectic considers nature not as a state of rest and immobility, of stagnation and of immutability, but as a state of unceasing movement and change, unceasing renewal and evolution." [28] In the commentary to the fourth thesis he adds that the process of evolution must be understood "not as a circular movement, as a simple repetition of what has been, but as a progressing movement, as an upward movement..., as an evolution from the simple to the complex, from a low phase to a higher

one..." [29] This means that three theses are put forward about evolution: everything is in motion; the movement is not circular, but linear; it is an upward movement leading towards more complex forms which are at the same time called better forms. So we are here faced with the typical optimistic evolutionism of the eighteenth and nineteenth centuries which found expression in the belief in unending progress.

Two elements only are not involved in this evolution. On the one hand matter which, as we have seen, is eternal and, on the other hand, the laws of evolution; for as Lenin says, "nothing is eternal except matter and the laws governing its evolution". [30] "The law is a reflection of that which is real in the movement of the universe" [31] (in other words the reflection of the real relationships mentioned by Hegel). It is deduced from this that this law has an objective and absolute character. [32] But this absolute character must be understood in the 'dialectical' way; it does not exclude relativity nor the dependence of the laws on historical conditions. [33] Not only is the law inevitably "restricted..., incomplete, approximate" which "applies only to the static and the unchangeable, to that which remains in a state of rest" [34]; but, more than this, even the firm element within that law depends for its applicability on the state of evolution at any given moment; for instance, the law which states that water remains liquid at temperatures between $0°$ and $100°$ is perhaps not applicable on the moon. [35] According to Lenin "the difference between the relative and the absolute is only relative" and there is an "element of relativity in the absolute". [36]

In order to avoid misunderstandings, two observations must be made here. 1] This doctrine is not identical with actualism; for, as we have seen, the substance of matter is preserved during the process of evolution. 2] Unlike Hegel, the dialectical materialists understand evolution in a strictly temporal sense; with Hegel at least some aspects of this evolution are timeless. But in the view of the dialectical materialists, nothing exists outside of time.

5. THE NATURE OF BECOMING: 1] CATEGORIAL PLURALISM. All that has been said about the nature of evolution could be said equally well of evolution as conceived by the classical evolutionists like, for instance, Spencer's followers; at this point, however, there intrudes a fundamental doctrine, stemming from Hegel, which radically alters the interpretation of the word. "Dialectic", writes Stalin, "unlike metaphysics,

views the process of evolution not as a simple process of growth in which changes of quantity do not lead to changes of quality; on the contrary, the dialectic views it as an evolution which starts with insignificant and invisible quantitative changes and moves over to apparent changes, fundamental and qualitative changes, an evolution in which qualitative changes occur not gradually but rapidly, suddenly, in the form of a spasmodic transition from one state to another, not fortuitously but according to certain laws, as the outcome of the accumulation of imperceptible and gradual quantitative changes".[37] We have already spoken of necessity; this last quotation, which summarizes the Marxist-Leninist doctrine exceedingly well, contains three theses, apart from affirming this inevitability: 1] qualitative changes do take place; 2] these changes take place in 'leaps'; 3] the 'leap' is the result of quantitative changes.

1] Dialectical Materialism admits of the existence of various qualities; in this it disagrees radically with classical materialism (called 'vulgar' by the Communists) and with Spencer's philosophy. Spencer maintained that the different phases of existence differ only in the more or less complex arrangement of particles of matter in time and space and under the influence of mechanical forces. This conception is not that of Dialectical Materialism. According to the latter there is a 'radical' difference between, for instance, crude matter and life, life and consciousness, perception and notion, the capitalist and the socialist systems; this is a qualitative difference. The world is not uniform but is made up of several phases of being. This doctrine is called "categorial pluralism" in contemporary philosophy.

Now, what is understood by the term 'quality'? According to Hegel, quality *(kačestvo)* differs from property *(svojstvo)* in that it defines the thing directly while the property defines its relations with other things.[38] Leonov defined quality as the "wholeness *(celostnost')* of the thing: the foundation *(osnova)* of all the properties of the thing"[39]; but this thesis could not stand up under criticism.[40] At any rate, quality is inseparable from its bearer: "If quality is removed, then the object itself ceases to exist".[41] From this it is possible to conclude that qualities are the real determinations of things. On the other hand, quantity, *(količestvo)*, which, in Hegel's[42] view, is an external determination referring to the being of a thing, is defined by Dialectical Materialism as follows: "quantity is a determination which is not identical *(tožestvenny)* with the object to the extent that the object itself does not cease to exist directly its quantitative changes."[43] From this one can conclude that for the dialectical materialists 'quality' and 'quantity' are roughly the same, respectively, as the 'essential attribute' and the 'accidental attribute' were for the Scholastics. What Dialectical Materialism teaches here could therefore be formulated in the terminology of Scholasticism as the fact that evolution produces essentially new forms.

6. THE NATURE OF BECOMING: 2] THE DIALECTICAL 'LEAP'. The thesis of the phases of being is expressed even more pointedly in the doctrine of the 'leap' *(skačok)*; this 'leap' represents a dissolution, a sudden transition into another quality. Thus water moves suddenly from the liquid into a solid or a gazeous state [44]; thus a given structure of society changes into another by means of revolution. [45] A few points need further elucidation. First of all, one must not imagine the 'leap' independently of time; as we know, all movement is bound up with time; the only difference is that the movement in the 'leap' itself takes place exceedingly fast. [46] Also, not the whole amount of water evaporates simultaneously. Engels says: "To be quite accurate, there are no 'leaps' in nature, because nature consists of nothing but 'leaps'."[47] "What science tries to find out are the stages, the gradations within the 'leap' and it is the triumph of theoretical and of applied science to have discovered them".[48] Just as there are different phases of being, so there are different kinds of 'leaps'.[49] It is even said that a new quality arises suddenly. There is obviously to be found here the possibility of applying this theory, for instance, to the theory of mutation in biology or to the socialist theory of revolution. But we must point out specifically that the Communists insist that they are not supporters of the theory of the 'leap' because they are revolutionaries; on the contrary, they insist that they are revolutionaries and believe that a change in the social order by evolution alone is impossible *because* they believe in Dialectical Materialism with its theory of the 'leap'.[50] Here we should like to point out once again the resemblance between the theory of the dialectical 'leap' and the Thomistic theory of 'substantial' becoming; this theory even goes so far as to teach that such becoming takes place in a single instant. [51]

Finally, – and this is our third thesis – this 'leap' is prepared and caused by a slow accumulation of quantitative changes; according to the already quoted definition of quantity and quality, this means that the accumulation of accidental changes at a given moment becomes a real change in the nature of a thing. We now can say that the revolutionary theory of the dialectical 'leap' does not exclude evolution but actually demands it; a relatively long period of evolution (quantitative aspect) is required to prepare the revolution, the 'leap' into a new order of society (qualitative aspect).

7. THE 'CONFLICT' OF THE OPPOSITES. Stalin's fourth law emphasizes yet further the revolutionary character of the dialectic: "In opposition to metaphysics, the dialectic takes its departure from the fact that internal conflicts are inherent in all natural things, in all natural phenomena, that they all have a negative and a positive side, a past and a future, a side which is dying and one which is developing; dialectic starts from the fact that the struggle between these opposites, the struggle between the old and the new, between what is dying and what is just forming, between what is decaying and what is developing, gives meaning to the sudden transformation of quantitative into qualitative changes". [52] This doctrine contains three essential components: 1] things contain opposites; 2] these opposites represent that which is old and decaying and that which is new and rising; 3] the struggle between these antagonistic elements forms the inmost kernel of evolution. These theses are a summary of a passage taken from Lenin's *Notebooks* [51] which is of basic importance here.
1] The 'opposites' are elucidated by Lenin in the following examples; + and —, differential and integral, action and reaction, positive and negative electricity, the combination and the disintegration of atoms, the class struggle". [53] These are obviously not contradictory opposites as Engels, who evidently did not know the elements of formal logic, thought but opposites of a different kind. Lenin sometimes used a word meaning "standing in opposition to", but he too understood one and the same thing under 'contrary' and 'contradictory'. He even spoke of the "identity of contrary opposites" [54], but it is obvious that there cannot be true identity here. He even added that it "might be more correct to speak of unity", saying: "in a certain sense both (expressions) are correct" [55] – which certainly is not true. For instance, if two social classes fight against each other, they may be united within a society but they are certainly not identical. It is evident that this badly formulated thesis really means

the following: there are in things certain factors and aspects which are in opposition one to the other. Put this way, the statement is not only Hegelian but just trivial. When Lenin followed in Engels' footsteps he was equally obscure. For instance, he said specifically that the association of the individual and the general in our judgment is an 'identity'; but, when he came to explain this identity in greater detail, he spoke of an 'association' of the two.[56] The other dialectical materialists are even more obscure.

One feature of antithesis, which is extremely important in Hegel's doctrine and which Lenin adopted, was not mentioned by Stalin in his summary; the 'contradictory' factors are not only in opposition to one another, but they also determine one another just as one magnetic pole cannot be conceived without the other.

2] If all that is, is also in the process of becoming, it inevitably follows that opposing factors are not static; Lenin deduced from this that one of the factors is a decaying element while another one develops at its expense. This is what he called the 'struggle' of the opposites, incidentally putting the word in inverted commas. This struggle will follow a different course according to the dialectical level at which it takes place. According to Ždanov's speech, one can distinguish, at the present moment, an 'antagonistic' struggle (for instance in the class struggle) and a non-antagonistic one (for instance that peaceful opposition which according to these authors is in progress in Soviet Russia – in spite of the Vavilov case!). The 'Programme'[57], too, devotes a paragraph to this opposition; but Leonov has not worked it out yet, for which he is blamed even though his critics themselves can give no indication as to how a struggle can be conceived which is not 'antagonistic'. All we learn is that the 'struggle' must now assume the form of 'criticism and self-criticism'.

The following should also be noted: while the Russian dialectical materialists do not explain this classification of the opposites and exhaust themselves in repeating Stalin's words and in accumulating examples [58], Mao Tse-tung has, it would seem, provided a theory which fits Lenin's thought. He states that in an 'opposition' both its universality and its particularity should be considered; its universality because it is to be found everywhere; its particularity because in every sphere it assumes a different form. [59]

3] This opposition or struggle is immanent "in the very essence of things". [60]

This is a fundamental thesis in the system taken as a whole. Lenin says that by means of it the autodynamism *(samodviženie)* of nature can be explained. In his view, movement does not emanate from an external source, is not 'caused' by a factor operating from outside, but has its origin in the very nature of things. And so it can be said that movement is an essential property of matter; this implies the anti-theological consequences which we have described. [61]

8. SUMMARY: LENIN'S 16 POINTS. According to Stalin, the objective dialectic could be summarized as follows: it is a doctrine which says that the opposition, immanent in the very nature of things, is the motive power for the general deterministic development which takes place in 'leaps' in a world which is a dynamic entity, thanks to the inter-connection between everything that exists. This is a Hegelian doctrine in which the influence of materialism is not very apparent. It will be useful to quote a page from Lenin's *Philosophical Notebooks* [62] which illustrates very well the relative importance of the separate elements in Lenin's dialectic. These can be formulated as follows:

"1. objectivity of observation (... the thing itself);

2. integral sum of the multiple relationships between this thing and others;

3. evolution of this thing;

4. the tendencies (and aspects) of the thing;

5. the thing as sum and union of the opposites;

6. the struggle *around* the unfolding of these opposites;

7. the association of analysis and synthesis, the destruction of the parts, the sum total of these parts;

8. ...everything is once again joined to *every* other thing;

9. transitions from *every* determination, quality, feature, appearance, property to every other;

10. an unending process revealing ever *new* phenomena;

11. an unending process of ever deepening knowledge of a thing... on the part of man moving from the phenomenon to the essence, from the shallower to the deeper essence;

12. from co-existence to causality;

13. at a higher phase the repetition of certain features, properties, etc. of the lower phase;

14. return almost to the primitive stage (negation of negation);
15. struggle of content against form, stripping off of the form, transformation of the content;
16. transition from quantity to quality and vice versa."

Lenin considered the last two points merely as illustrations of point 9; in this he disagreed with Engels [63] who considered the transition from quantity to quality as one of the three great laws of dialectic. An interesting feature of this analysis is the fact that Hegel's synthesis plays a very subordinate part here; Stalin does not even mention it. Certainly modern dialectical materialists do not reject synthesis, but the essential for them is the struggle, the destruction of the old by the new.

9. THE FOUNDATIONS OF DIALECTIC. The Communists never prove the majority of the important theses of their dialectic. When Sviderskij called upon Leonov to provide a proof for various of these theses [64], he was criticized for wanting to have answers to 'sterile' questions which were not to be discussed [65]. If proof is given for certain dialectical statements, this always happens in Engels' superficial manner with the adduction of examples from natural science and social science (North Pole – South Pole; class struggle, etc.). It is quite unnecessary to investigate this any closer. It will, however, be interesting to examine what connection there is between this doctrine and Lenin's conception of the world. Such a connection seems to exist at three different levels; hence the acceptance of dialectic by Lenin and his disciples.

First of all, Lenin was a socialist revolutionary. It is only natural that he should have accepted a doctrine which propounded the existence of a 'social' association of various elements of reality as well as its fluid nature; a doctrine which implanted the law of revolution into the very essence of being and which stated that the old must of necessity be eliminated. We have seen that *in the sphere of logic* the Bolsheviks deduced their revolutionary theories from the dialectic. But it is obvious that they accepted this dialectic for *psychological* reasons because it gave a theoretical foundation for revolution.

There was one other reason; Lenin's deep-rooted bent for engineering – which was discussed in the chapter on materialism. Dialectic is a godsend for a man of this type; just as are the doctrines of realism, rationalism and materialism. It supplied this very pronounced man of action with a theory in which priority was assigned to action and it revealed to him an unlimited field of action.

Finally, it is easy to understand that this dialectic proved a useful tool for the elimination of God: the theory of autodynamism *(samodviženie)* – according to Lenin an essential element of this doctrine – states that movement is the most essential property of matter and thereby makes it impossible for Dialectical Materialism to accept the existence of God. Here Lenin found another absolute; infinite, eternal matter in movement originating in itself; this is his god.

It is, therefore, with full justification that dialectic is called 'the soul of materialism': it is, in fact, its religion.

RFERENCES: [1] Encyclopaedia, Par. 11, p. 43. [2] Ib. par. 81, p. 105. [3] KFS 60a. [4] Pr 316; cf. Lenin, Voprosy 247. [5] MEM 467. [6] *Dial. Prirody* (in Russian) 125; cf. Mitin 1934, 140. [7] FT 211 et seq. [8] KFS 103a. [9] DM 143a; KFS 36a. [10] LF 52f. [11] Phänom. 21. [12] FT 125. [13] BAD 31; ME 165; KFS 73a. [14] ME 147 et seq. cf. Pr. 316a. [15] FT 156; KFS 219a; Pr 316a. [16] KFS 219a. [17] KFS 274a; cf. Mitin 1933, 197. [18] Lenin "What is to be done?", ed. WWI, 197 et seq.; KFS 266a. [19] KFS 188b. [20] DM 144. [21] BSE 21, 575; KFS 59a; Pr 316a. [22] KFS 188a; Leonov 1947, 70, 117 et seq. 23 BSE 22, 183. [24] AD 135 et seq.; BSE 41, 616; KFS 244a. [25] AD 306; BSE 41, 617. [26] Mitin 1933, 204. [27] KFS 32b. [28] DM 143(b). [29] DM 145(c). [30] KFS 160b. [31] FT 148. [32] KFS 77. [33] Leonov 1947, 88. [34] FT 148. [35] Mitin 1933, 189. [36] FT–ME 376. [37] DM 144(c). [38] BSE 22, 155. [39] Leonov 1947, 140. [40] P. C. Trofimov, VF 1948, I, 295a. [41] KFS 104b. [42] Encyklopaedia, Par. 99. p. 199. [43] KFS 112b. [44] AD 503. DM 145. [45] DM 149. [46] Trofimov op. cit. 294a. [47] AD 353. [48] Ya. P. Golenčenko, VF 1947, I, 314. [49] KFS 250a. [50] DM 147. [51] J. Gredt: *Elementa philosophiae Aristotelico-Thomisticae*, Friburgi Br. 1926, 298 et seq. [52] DM 147. [53] FT–ME 375. [54] Ib. [55] Ib. [56] FT–ME 377. [57] Pr. 317b. [58] See, for instance, M. Rozental' 1954, 274 et seq., 288 et seq. [59] On contrad. 10–39. [60] FT 263. [61] KFS 54b. [62] FT 211 et seq. [63] *Dial. Prirody* 125 et seq., cf. Mitin 1933, 140. [64] Sviderskij 306a. [65] Trofimov op. cit. 296b.

IX. METHODOLOGY: APPLICATIONS

I. SUBJECTIVE DIALECTIC. In spite of what Stalin said about it, dialectic is, as we have said already, first and foremost an ontology, i.e. a theory of being; it is, to a lesser degree, also a methodology; furthermore it is applied to psychological and epistemological problems with results which deeply transform certain theses which can be drawn from materialism.

Indeed, dialectic is also an epistemological theory as well as a system of logic. [1] This close association of objective dialectic (ontology) and of subjective dialectic (methodology, etc.) is easy to understand in the case of Hegel, for he makes no distinction between being and thinking; in Dialectical Materialism a justification for it is given in the theory of reflection which states that thinking is an image of being.

However, in spite of all the praise it has earned, the direct application of dialectic in methodology remains one of the weakest aspects of Dialectical Materialism. The following theses will show just how it is applied: 1] as phenomena are inter-related "no single phenomenon in nature can be understood if it is taken in isolation". [2] And so the first rule runs as follows: phenomena should be observed in such a way as to give due consideration to their environment. 2] Since everything that is, is the result of the process of becoming and is still involved in this process, "the dialectical method requires that the phenomena be... considered not only from the point of view of their mutual interconnections and interdependence but also from the point of view of their movements, their changes, their development". [3] Since, in the process of evolution, the new replaces the old, "particular importance should be attached, not to that which seems to be firm at any given moment while it is already beginning to wither away, but to that which is in process of formation, which is evolving..." [4]; in other words the future of things should above all be taken into account; it is a kind of teleological method that is propounded here.

In this methodology there is much talk of the application of the law of inner contradictions, but it is quite impossible to draw from it a sufficiently clear and useful methodological law; and no wonder, for according to dialectic itself the opposition between these "contradictory" factors is different at every level, if not in every individual case. Engels observed already that "to destroy a grain of corn" did not mean the same as to "negate it dialectically"; for the latter, one has to sow it in the ground. [5] In these conditions no philosophy can possibly establish a general methodological law.

2. THEORY AND PRACTICE. There is no doubt that great methodological importance attaches to the thesis which claims that opposites are intimately connected and that they deeply influence each other. This applies particularly to the doctrine of the unity of theory and practice.

Already Marx assigned very great importance to practice. His eleventh thesis on Feuerbach says: "All that the philosophers have done is to devise various interpretations of the world; what is important, though, is to change it".[6] Lenin and the Leninists attributed even greater importance to this thesis. The unity of practice and theory is founded on this thesis. Practice is in fact the opposite of theory, therefore one deeply influences the other. Here is the source of various principles important in methodology, epistemology and practice.

We have already stated that for realism practice is the criterion of truth. Marx even went so far as to say: the question whether human thought is capable of attaining objective truth is not a theoretical but a practical one.[7] We have also seen how Lenin assents to and defends Engels' well-known argument against the existence of Kant's 'thing in itself'. Apart from being the criterion for the realistic doctrine in general, practice is also the criterion for every individual apprehension of knowledge. Lenin says: "Human thought is 'economic' only when it reflects objective truth correctly and the criterion of this correctness is practice, experiment, industry".[8]

Finally, knowledge arises out of practice. Here, as an illustration, is a dialectic with thesis, antithesis and synthesis: "The path from living observation to abstract thought and from the latter to practice, that is the dialectical path of the recognition of truth".[9] We might also quote Mitin: "In practice is realized the union of subject and object. Man transforms himself by acting upon nature".[60]

Here is to be sought the explanation of various, otherwise almost inexplicable, phenomena apparent in Soviet philosophy; for instance, its exaggerated acclamation of politicians as great philosophers, the stressing of the political character of all philosophy, the long chapters in the 'Programme'[11] on the importance of philosophy and finally the importance ascribed to philosophy itself in Soviet practice and the stressing of its importance as a 'weapon'. The significance of these phenomena, and of practice in general, becomes properly comprehensible only in the light of Historical Materialism.

3. APPLICATION TO SCIENCE. References in Soviet Russia are constantly made to fruitful applications of the dialectical method to science. For instance, S. I. Vavilov, the president of the Academy of

Sciences of the USSR, (not to be confused with N. I. Vavilov, Lysenko's victim) says that "the Soviet scientists, armed with the method of Dialectical Materialism, courageously combat the crude falsifications of science by the bourgeois scientists" [12]; he also underlines the fact that Dialectical Materialism forms the basis for the Academy's activities. [13] But, in actual fact, we have been unable to find *one single way* in which the dialectical *method* has been applied to natural science; on the other hand, its *ontological* theses are constantly being applied to various sciences.

In this context it is interesting to point out two facts: 1] Since 1922, Einstein's theory of relativity has been rejected by Soviet scientists and 25 years have been needed for an acceptable 'dialectical' interpretation of this theory to be found; even this interpretation, however, does not find everything in physics acceptable. Thus Ždanov declared, in 1947, that the "finitistic" theory (which claims that the universe is finite in time and space) and Milne's calculations were 'anti-dialectical', that Eddington's physical constants were 'Pythagorean mysticism' and that the attempt to explain matter as a totality of waves was a 'devilish notion – *(čertovščina)*'.[14] 2] In economics Soviet thinkers claimed that the revolution was a dialectical 'leap' and felt it necessary to reject the notion of value; after thirty years they have now moved away from this position and have found a "dialectical" interpretation of value.[15] 3] The best known illustration is to be found in genetics. We shall not examine in detail. T. D. Lysenko's views (responsible for the suppression of the Mendelians) which were received very coolly by specialists in the Marxist camp. [16] It will suffice to say here that the discussion was based partly on philosophical arguments and the opponents were accused of being prepared to support the idea of the immutability of the genes, i.e. an anti-dialectical doctrine. [17] Similar situations are to be found in many other branches of science.

We saw in Chapter V, 5 and 6, what catastrophic results the application of dialectic to psychology and logic had engendered. It can be said without exaggeration that everything positive that Russian science has achieved (and that is a great deal since 1917) was achieved not *because of* but *in spite of* the application of dialectic. Wherever an attempt was made to apply dialectic, the result was inhibiting, if not actually destructive, of scientific research.

REFERENCES: [1] FT–ME 377; Pr. 316a. [2] DM 143 et seq. [3] Ibid. [4] DM 144. [5] Cf. Walter 1947, 69. [6] LF 76. [7] Thesen über Feuerbach II, LF 73 et seq. [8] ME 162. [9] FT 166. [10] Mitin 1934, 128 et seq. [11] Pr 313b, 317. [12] Vavilov 1948(I), 117. [13] Vavilov 1946, 427. [14] Žd 271. [15] See Feuer 118. [16] Fyfe 1947; see also Feuer 119. [17] O položenii: Lysenko pp. 13, 20, Mitin p. 232 et seq.

X. HISTORICAL MATERIALISM

Our research is mainly concerned with *Dialectical* Materialism and not with Historical Materialism which represents the application of the former to the phenomena of life in society. [1] In the latter we find a number of theses which, in their majority, belong not to philosophy but to sociology in general. But, as certain aspects of Dialectical Materialism are not fully comprehensible unless one considers Historical Materialism at the same time, we shall give a quick sketch of the latter according to Stalin [2]; we shall then study the conclusions which are to be drawn from it and which pertain directly or indirectly to the real subject of our investigation, namely Dialectical Materialism.

I. ITS FOUNDATIONS. Historical Materialism has its foundations in that psychological thesis of materialism which states that "nature, being, the material world are primary..., whereas consciousness, thought are secondary and derived from the former...". [3] This is the theory from which Lenin and, following in his footsteps, Stalin first derived their theory of reflection which states that consciousness and mind in general are a reflection of the perceived object. Thus they interpret the notions 'nature', 'being', 'material world' as objects to be apprehended by knowledge. However, it can also be interpreted in another way; one can understand by the same words not the object but the body of the subject as well. Thereupon consciousness becomes no longer the reflection of objective reality external to man, but the reflection of that which takes place in his body. This is the interpretation which serves as basis for the thesis of Dialectical Materialism which claims that thought is either a function, a product or a concomitant of matter, i.e. of the human body. Now the same interpretation serves as a basis for 'Historical' Materialism. Stalin said that if the above-mentioned thesis is true, "the conclusion can

98

be drawn from it that the material life of society and its being is that which is primary, original in it and that its spiritual life is secondary, derived from it..., but that the spiritual life of society is a reflection image *(otraženie)* of this reality, a reflected image of its being". [4] In other words, just as the spiritual life of the individual is a reflection of his physical life, so the spiritual life of society is a reflection of its material life.

Therefore, Stalin concluded, "the sources of spiritual life must be sought in the material circumstances of the life of society, in the essence of society, whose image is reflected by these ideas, theories, views, etc." [5] This is the fundamental principle of Historical Materialism.

2. SKETCH OF THE THEORY. By "material circumstances of the life of society" Stalin did not mean the geographical factors [6] nor the demographic ones [7] which are admittedly 'circumstances' but not the determining ones *(opredeljajuščie)*. The principal factor which sets its imprint on society is the method by which this society obtains its livelihood. [8] Two elements can be found in this method: on the one hand, the productive forces *(proizvoditel'nye sily)* and, on the other, the conditions of production *(proizvodstvennye otnošenija)* as they affect men. Four factors make up the productive forces: the means of production, the men who operate them, know-how and efficiency. The order in which they are listed seems to be intentional: the nature of the tool forms man; only then do know-how and efficiency become operative. All productive work is social; work alone calls forth mutual relationships among men; these relationships depend on productive forces. [9]

Production has three characteristic features: 1] it is always in the process of changing. [10] 2] The change always begins with a change in the instruments of production; influenced by, and in accord with, changes in these instruments all the other factors change too, including conditions of production. [11] 3] The new forces and conditions of production begin to form already in the bosom of the old society [12]; for men are not free to choose this or that method of production and even while improving their instruments of production they do not realize what results in the life of society these improvements must bring in their train. [13] There are four main stages in the development of productive forces and five basic types *(formacija)* of conditions of production: 1] conditions of primitive community life (stone tools and the bow and arrow), 2] slavery (metal tools), 3] feudalism (plough and weaver's loom), 4] capitalism (machines), 5] socialism (large-scale mechanized industry). [14]

Productive forces and conditions of production, in the narrow sense (as distinct from the juridical or political system), form the economic base *(bazis)* of society. [15] This base determines directly the nature of the juridical and political superstructure *(nadstrojka)* [16] and indirectly the nature of the remaining superstructure, the 'ideology', e.g., morality, science, art, religion, philosophy. [17] This whole superstructure is no more than the reflected image of the base; to quote Stalin [18]: as men live, so do they think. Therefore, for every method of production there is a corresponding system of social ideals, a specific ideology: thus the philosophy of the ancients is the expression of the ancient economic system, Scholastic philosophy the reflected image of feudalism and Dialectical Materialism that of the modern economic epoch.

Complications are engendered by the class struggle. [19] According to Lenin a class is a group of human beings characterized by their position in a historical system conditioned by social production, by their relations to the means of production, by their rôle in the organization of society and by their method of appropriation, i.e. their manner of participating in the income of the community. [20] During the first period (primitive community) there are no classes; nor will there be any in the last one (socialism); during all the intermediate periods there exist an exploited class (slaves, serfs, wage-earners) and an exploiting class (slave-owners, feudal lords, capitalists).

In this context the principal thesis, which is not at all easy to prove, states that the classes personify, so to speak, the different periods: thus the capitalists personify the fourth period while the wage earners, the proletariat, personify the fifth. It follows from this that every class has its own ideology. [21]

3. THE IMPORTANCE OF IDEAS: PRAGMATISM. Therefore, as regards the origins of social ideas, the situation is as follows: these ideas are merely reflected images of the life society, of social classes. The factors which, when all is said and done, really exert a determining influence on them are the instruments of production; they determine the life of society and its structure. But one must not conclude from this that ideas have lost all importance. In this connection Stalin quotes Marx: "Theory

becomes material power as soon as it seizes hold of the masses"[22], and he adds: "So far as the importance of social ideas, theories, views... and their rôle in history is concerned, Historical Materialism not only does not question their very weighty rôle and importance in the life of society but, on the contrary, stresses it".[23]

For, ideas are the tools of life: "When all is said and done, new ideas and theories arise just because they are necessary for society".[24] Social ideas, therefore, do not only correspond to material conditions (i.e., to the method of production of a given society), but they also serve society, viz., the ruling class of society. That is why they exist. We are here faced with true pragmatism; a social idea is considered right not because it corresponds to objective reality but because it is a good tool for the class which has brought it forth. Therefore, as we shall see, 'objective' social ideas do not exist; on the contrary, every social idea is a class affair, it is good for *one* class and bad for another.

But what is understood by the expression 'social ideas'? In the passages which we have quoted, this term covers all ideas which belong to 'ideology'; i.e. political, juridical, scientific, philosophical, religious ideas. Stalin was particularly careful about qualifying the word 'idea' with the adjective 'social' when he applied the pragmatic principle. One might get the impression that there is a twofold theory of truth; the pragmatic one for social ideas and the realistic one for the others. Despite the wording, this is not so. For both the social ideas themselves and thinking in general are covered by the word 'social'. Judin and Rozental', in the article 'Thinking', say: "Human thinking is a social phenomenon and cannot be comprehended apart from the history of society".[25] This doctrine stems from Engels, according to whom work has fashioned man and determines his thinking to a substantial extent.[26] And work, as we have seen, is always a social activity. Pragmatism, therefore, in Historical Materialism is, after all, generally applicable and is not restricted to social doctrines.*

In the light of this doctrine the relationship between theory and practice finally becomes clear and well-defined. We have seen already that practice is the criterion of realism and truth in general and that theory is dialectically associated with it. But here it is no longer merely a question of a simple dialectical association; here absolute primacy of practice is taught. Theory is engendered by practice and is merely its tool; "the primary and fundamental epistemological standpoint must always be the practical one, the one based on life"[27]; and, as is to be deduced from the totality of the doctrine, this must be the point of view of all knowledge.

4. THE PARTISAN CHARACTER OF PHILOSOPHY. Only now are we properly prepared to understand one of the most paradoxical theses of Communist philosophers; namely that science and philosophy are, and must be, intimately associated with the Party *(partijnost')* and that, therefore, every neutral, objective and apolitical attitude is condemned. Lenin has said, "people belonging to no party are hopeless bunglers in philosophy just as much as they are bunglers in politics". [28] In its context this sentence is, it is true, directed only against the pseudo-philosophers who want to retain their neutrality between realism and idealism, but Lenin also said, "modern philosophy is just as 'partisan' today as it was 2000 years ago". [29] This statement has never been questioned by the Communists. In fact, in 1932, L. Žvonov devoted an entire book to it; and it is treated in a special article in Judin and Rozental' 's dictionary. [30] Ždanov calls objectivity 'toothless vegetarianism' [31] and criticizes Aleksandrov for having been insufficiently partisan in his *History of Philosophy*. [32] No wonder then that the 'Programme' contains a special section on the 'partisanship of philosophy' [33] and that the scientists are reproached with increasing frequency for being 'objective' and 'apolitical'. We have seen already that the logicians were condemned for their neutrality. [34] No better fate seems to be awaiting the psychologists, for "Bolshevik party spirit" is demanded of them when dealing with "problems of psychology". [35] There is a long study of this subject by M. D. Kammari. [36] More examples could be given. Indeed, the fight against the apolitical and objective character of philosophy seems to be one of the most important features of Communist philosophy today.

This is inevitable, for Communist philosophy claims that it is the social

---

* It is true that since 1950 (when Stalin declared that language was not a function of a class) this principle has been breached with growing frequency; as regards social doctrine, this is also true. An example of this is provided by the new doctrine (referred to in Chapter V, 5) which states that logic is a general human activity. The same seems to be valid for certain spheres in all natural sciences. Thus a fundamental principle of Historical Materialism has been cast aside, apparently in view of practical requirements (atomic research, etc.) and of the truly scientific attitude of the physicists, etc.

doctrine of the Communist Party which, in its turn, claims to be the party of the proletariat. Philosophy is a weapon in the Party's fight and so could not possibly be either neutral or objective.

There are difficulties, however; if objectivism is rejected, what happens to the principles of realism which are so heavily stressed in Dialectical Materialism? How can these two doctrines be reconciled? Two attempts at reconciliation are to be found in Soviet literature; one by N. Bukharin and a more recent one by M. D. Kammari. The former is by a philosopher who was condemned (both as a 'mechanist' and as a 'monster'); it cannot, therefore, be considered orthodox. The latter, on the other hand, was published in *Voprosy* immediately after Ždanov's speech and under very strict supervision; it can, therefore, be considered as an expression of the official point of view at the time. Bukharin specifically asked himself "why proletarian science stands higher than bourgeois science" and replied that this is so, because the bourgeois, busily engaged in maintaining the established order of things, have a restricted horizon while the proletariat, longing for revolution, look much further. [37] Kammari's reply was sharper and more penetrating. After all, the fact that philosophy is partisan does not mean that it is subjective.[38] Marxism looks at all phenomena perfectly objectively, scientifically.[39] But the term 'objective' does not mean that one stands above all classes and above history; the bourgeois who claim that they do this, camouflage their class interests with this statement. As long as classes exist, there can be no 'non-partisan' philosophy.[40] And so Marxist philosophy is partisan. But its partisanship is identical with an objective view of the nature of cognition; in other words, Marxism alone knows what the true nature of cognition is. [41] For, Marxism pursues the interests of the proletariat and serves them; by doing this it moves in the same direction as objective history itself and for the true good of science, for the interests of the proletariat are identical with those of history.

So much for the principle of partisanship and its justification in Communist philosophy. It is clear that this philosophy specifically proclaims itself to be not a non-partisan science but a useful weapon in the class struggle. As we have seen, this seems to be applicable not only to philosophy but also to all of man's intellectual activity.

5. THE PARTISAN CHARACTER OF MORALITY, ART AND RELIGION.
As the study of Historical Materialism is not our prime concern, we shall

investigate briefly how this principle of partisanship operates in various other fields.

On *morality* Lenin had said the following: "The struggle for the strengthening and perfecting of Communism is immanent in the nature of Communist morality *(nravstvennost')*". [42] An extremely utilitarian interpretation is given of morality: "Ethical and moral is only that which contributes to the destruction of the old world, to the abolition of exploitation and of poverty, and that which supports the new socialistic social order". [43] At present particular importance is attached to the second part of this sentence. The 1948 Programme contained a special chapter on socialist solidarity [44] which, it claimed, is required for the establishment of the new order; the pedagogues too, as we have seen, devoted much attention to this problem. [45] However, morality is a function of class, not only in bourgeois society, where it is used for exploiting the working man [46], but also quite as much in a socialist state where, on the contrary, it represents the higher ethics of the working class. [47]

Thanks to Gorky's authority, *aesthetics* has always been the section of axiology which was viewed with most favour. This too, however, is the concern of the Party: the project of the programme for aesthetics, published in 1948, contained not only a paragraph, but a whole chapter "on partisanship and ideology *(idejnost')* as essential features of Soviet art". [48] Art is a form of social cognition [49]; but it is also, and to an equal extent, a reflection *(otraženie)* of reality. [50] This does not prevent the beautiful which it expresses from being "a reflection of the ideals of various classes" [51]. In Soviet art the beautiful is a reflection of "the struggle of the Soviet nation". [52] This art should be 'socialist' in content, national in form. [53] No wonder then that in his summary of the discussion on Soviet aesthetics M. M. Rozental' should conclude that the first duty of Soviet aesthetics is "the fight against decadent and bourgeois aesthetics, against formalism and naturalism... against cosmopolitanism, against servility *(nizkopoklonstvo)* towards non-Russians, against objectivity, against non-partisanship *(bespartijnost')* in all works by Soviet critics". [54] We cannot embark here upon an analysis of what is meant by 'socialist realism' in Soviet Russia; but, in spite of the violent rejection of 'bourgeois utilitarianism' in art [55], one cannot but observe that Soviet aesthetics are profoundly socio-utilitarian.

Finally, *religion* is considered, on the one hand, as a pseudo-science, as the epitome of erroneous theoretical theses and, on the other, as an instrument for the exploitation of the worker by the bourgeois. It is impossible here to analyse these familiar theories any deeper; they lie beyond the scope of our investigation. We want to make only one further observation; unlike all other sets of values, religion is to disappear in the socialist system. Lunačarskij, it is true, had considered, with more logic than one might think, that every system ought to have its own religion just as it has its own philosophy, science, morality, art, etc.; but Lenin had fought this conception most energetically [56] and Lenin's doctrine still holds sway. To prove this it suffices to refer to the publication of Lenin's selected works, *Marx-Engels-Marxism* in 1947, which contain two of his most violent anti-religious works: *The Attitude of the Workers' Party Towards Religion* [57] and *The Tasks of Militant Materialism*. [58] The Programme, too, contains a paragraph entitled 'The Importance of Philosophical Marxist Materialism in the Fight against Religion and Superstition in all its Forms'. [59]

Be it noted that these principles are still operative today, and quite unaltered. Thus in the July 1956 issue of *Voprosy Filosofii* N. I. Gubanov reviewed numerous 'scientific-atheistic' works of popularization and began his review by asserting that this was a very important educational action. [60] The tactics of the Party in regard to religion may change but its principles remain the same.

In conclusion, the following can be said of the Communist doctrine of values: 1] religious values are simply negated; 2] aesthetic values are not rejected outright but they are subordinated to moral ones; 3] moral values are considered for their utilitarian worth. At first sight, therefore, we might have the impression that we have here a radically relativistic, socio-utilitarian doctrine which acknowledges no absolute values and which, accordingly, describes all sets of values as functions of technical activity. But this is *not* the case. It is true that Historical Materialism denies every *finite* value and attributes only relative importance to all such sets of values, but this only means that the value in question is considered as a *means* to an end and is viewed in relation to something else. This something can, in its turn, be made relative to something else, and so on; but this argument cannot be carried on *ad infinitum*. If a value is considered relative, it must, when all is said and done, be considered relative to an absolute value. This applies to Historical Materialism also. An absolute value *does exist* according to this doctrine: class victory is an absolute value or, in concrete terms, the victory of the Communist Party. Now this victory, according to Historical Materialism, is the victory of human progress, and human progress is the highest phase of progress in general. This progress, in other words the progress of dialectic, represents for Communism the only absolute value. We have here, therefore, not a nihilistic conception of value (unlimited relativism of value) but a *monistic* one.

If one asks oneself what the nature of this solitary Communist concept of value is, it becomes apparent that it is a *religious* value. Dialectic is infinity and it is infinitely valuable. It – and consequently the Party – requires a palpably *sacramental* approach; the absolute concept of value demands unconditional self-sacrifice and unconditional application of all one's energy. This value is considered so absolute that in comparison to its absolute character all other values become relative, i.e. are negated.

REFERENCES: [1] DM 141. [2] DM 154–179. [3] DM 155. [4] Ibid. [5] DM 156. [6] DM 160. [7] DM 161 [8] DM 162; Pr 321a. [9] DM 162 et seq. [10] DM 164; Pr 320a. [11] DM 165. [12] DM 174; Pr 320a-b. [13] DM 175. [14] DM 168 et seq. [15] KFS 20 et seq.; Pr 321. [16] DM 178; Pr 324. [17] KFS 20a; Pr 325a. [18] DM 164; Pr 325a. [19] Pr 322. [20] KFS 108a. [21] Pr 324b. [22] DM 158. [23] DM 157; Pr 325b. [24] DM 158. [25] KFS 179b. [26] Ibid. [27] KFS 275 (*Sočinenija* 14, 130). [28] ME 289. [29] KFS 210. [30] KFS 210a. [31] Žd 201b. [32] Žd 201 et seq. [33] Pr 325a. [34] Osmakov 376b. [36] Maslina 334 et seq. [36] Kammari 84 et seq. [37] Bucharin 1927, 11 et seq. [38] Kammari 85a. [39] ibid. [40] Kammari 85a. [41] Ibid. [42] KFS 177b. [43] Ibid.; printed without any amendments in the fourth edition (1954), p. 366b. [44] Pr 326b. [45] See Chapter V. [46] Pr 325a. [47] Pr 326b. [48] Berestnev-Trofimov 322a–b. [49] Ibid. 341b. [50] Ibid. 342. [51] Ibid. 343b. [52] Ibid. 345a. [54] Zadači 291b. [55] Berestnev-Trofimov 341b. [56] ME 354. [57] MEM 239–244. [58] MEM 466–476. [59] Pr 320b. [60] VF 1956, 3, 210–214.

XI. THE VALUE OF DIALECTICAL MATERIALISM AS A THEORY

We will conclude our investigation with some critical observations about present-day Russian Dialectical Materialism. First of all we shall examine it from our own point of view; i.e., substantially in the light of the principles concerning content and method which are valid in the West; then

VALUE OF DIALECTICAL MATERIALISM

we shall ask ourselves about sociological relativity and its limits in order
to determine the extent to which our conclusions can lay claim to universal validity.

I. POSITIVE ELEMENTS. In our opinion Dialectical Materialism contains
a whole group of affirmations which are basically correct and which we
agree with. To this group belongs the thesis of the practical importance of
ideas and, particularly, of the importance of philosophy for life; many
'spiritualists' might even learn respect for speculative thought from the
Communists. Some truth also resides in the idea of *partijnost'*: one must
make decisions in philosophy, compromises and eclecticism are anti-
philosophical. Credit must also be given for surmounting positivism, for
placing philosophy in the position which befits it: philosophy is a discipline independent of the other sciences. It is by no means their servant,
but their ultimate basis.

In epistemology we are faced with a realism which rejects epistemological
idealism in all its aspects; we have here a healthy rationalism which rejects
all forms of relativism and frivolous scepticism and attributes to the mind
the ability to comprehend reality. In this particular point the Communists, quite unlike many superficial philosophers, have come to acknowledge essential realities *(die Wesenheiten)* and the possibility of their
being known.

In cosmology they reject categorial monism which reduces all phases of
being to a single fundamental form; similarly, one should acknowledge
the perfectly correct thesis that neither time nor space nor movement can
be conceived without a medium. These doctrines have enabled the dialectical materialists to establish a fundamentally correct psychology which
affirms the unity of man and which, in spite of its determinism, underlines
the importance of human will.

Dialectical Materialism contains an element of truth even in those of its
theses which we regard as much exaggerated. For instance, the Communists are quite justified in talking of the dependence of our entire
thought on environment and on history even though they exaggerate here
as they do everywhere else. Communism opposes those erroneous forms of
spiritualism which refuse to admit the influence of the body on the mind
and even if, here too, it goes too far, nevertheless its opposition to such
extreme spiritualism has some positive value. Of course, all these ideas

can also be found elsewhere, but Dialectical Materialism has the merit of insisting on these points with more force than many others. It can therefore be said that it indubitably contains a number of positive elements.

2. DIALECTICAL MATERIALISM AND COMMON SENSE. Now it is easy to perceive that Dialectical Materialism, so long as it deals with these elements, merely expresses truths which pertain to common sense, to the 'philosophy' of pre-philosophic man. Indeed, all the statements made in the preceding paragraph can be easily translated into the language of the man in the street. Wisdom is a useful thing; you must choose between black and white; whatever is true is absolutely true; we really do know something about the real world and can learn more about it; there is an essential difference between, for instance, man and stone; finally, the mind is somehow tied to the body. All these are accepted by common sense as self-evident truths – and justifiably so.

Even the affirmations of Dialectical Materialism which we reject as false are intimately connected with the everyday philosophy of pre-philosophic man. True, he finds no difficulty in accepting God, but it is equally true to say that often his thinking is fundamentally earth-bound and that he views with distrust any 'metaphysical system' which points to a beyond; in fact, he is often markedly materialistic. On the other hand, such a man is incapable of extricating himself from the apparent contradictions in reality; and dialectic comes obligingly to his aid with its affirmation that contradictions belong to reality. The average man finds something familiar even in the historicity and in the relativity by which so much store is set in the historical applications of the doctrine. To hold a belief in objective and absolute truth as well does not trouble him a bit; nor does it trouble Dialectical Materialism.

Dialectical Materialism contains, of course, other highly technical elements; especially those which have been taken over from Hegel – but these are mostly theses of marginal importance. The main doctrines are nothing but a robust and slightly systematized expression of simple common sense.

This feature constitutes the principal strength of Dialectical Materialism. Loyalty to common sense is the reason why it utters so many truths; for to this common sense belong truths which philosophers themselves cannot ignore if they want to avoid error. But here too lies one of the greatest weaknesses of the system.

3. TECHNICAL LEVEL OF THE PHILOSOPHERS. Before considering this question, we must refer to two differences: first, the difference between common sense and philosophy and, secondly, the difference between the truth of philosophical doctrines and their formulation. Indeed, these two differences are, nowadays, sometimes overlooked in the West.

First of all it is to be noted that philosophy is not identical with 'common sense'. It happens all too frequently that a man is termed a 'philosopher', especially if he is a physicist or even a poet, provided he speaks of the ultimate problems of existence and of man. There could hardly be a greater misnomer, for philosophy is a difficult *technical* discipline. Its methods and the nature of its problems have been evolved by outstanding thinkers and geniuses in 26 centuries of intensive work. Of course this work has not liquidated common sense, but it has analyzed its opinions more accurately, made them deeper and discovered subtle and complex problems beyond its generalized affirmations. True, philosophers differ on the solution and approach to many problems of philosophy. This results in a difference of technical level. When taken as a whole, European philosophy achieves a certain minimum technical level in the nature of the problems studied, in the methods and in the language – a minimum which is common to all philosophers. This level is always situated far above that of common sense.

Secondly, a sharp distinction must be drawn between the truth and the formulation of a philosophical doctrine. The same idea – whether it be true or false – can be well or badly expressed, it can make sense or not, it can be expressed in technically correct language or in an elementary way. It often happens in Western European philosophy that one disagrees with a doctrine and yet finds it interesting and worthy of investigation or refutation because it has been correctly formulated or because the problem has been correctly set out. In Western Europe a doctrine is termed 'philosophical' only when it displays, in this respect, a minimum of technical correctness; only such a doctrine is here considered scientific, whether one accepts it or not.

Let us now consider whether the term 'scientific', as defined above, can be applied to Dialectical Materialism. In other words, we are not concerned here with *truth,* but with the *technical level* of the range of problems set, of the methods of Dialectical Materialism and of its formulations. Let us see whether, in this sense, it can be considered a scientific philosophy.

The Communists give an affirmative answer to this question. They constantly extol their philosophy as being the only scientific philosophy and claim that the others have access only to a 'pseudo-science' devised, to the order of American imperialism or of the Vatican, with the intention of leading the proletariat astray and thus becoming better able to exploit it. Numerous Western authors support this claim by interpreting this Dialectical Materialism in accordance with its 'deeper intuitions' and by propounding this in a glistening and hazy language which hides its true face. Any attempt at a scientific analysis of this doctrine is rejected by them as being inapplicable which is all the more reason for not ignoring the technical criteria of philosophy and for applying its standards to the products of Communist thought.

4. DIALECTICAL MATERIALISM AS A SCIENCE. If the elementary criteria of philosophic technique and method are applied to Dialectical Materialism, one observes that the latter does not rise above the level of ordinary common sense: its technique, the range of its problems, and its formulations are abysmally primitive. What A. Pastore, who has much sympathy for Communism, said in the conclusion to his study of Lenin is equally applicable to Dialectical Materialism today: "No gnoseology, no metaphysics, no scientific competence, no psychology, no aesthetics, no ethics, no mysticism. A little – but very unsuccessful – epistemology, much use and abuse of Hegel's dialectic, no apparent systematic logic". Dialectical Materialism gives an exegesis of its 'classics' which is often subtle (though revelling in Hegelian verbosity), but the range of its problems, its formulations and its style of expression are incredibly primitive. More particularly, no true philosophical problem is ever set out clearly and correctly – let alone solved. It is not a philosophy, but rather a kind of atheistic catechism for believing members of the Party.

The truth of this could be demonstrated with reference to every separate question which Dialectical Materialism raises. We shall mention just a few. In logic there is a confusion between contradiction and the principle of the excluded middle, between contradictory and contrary opposites, between unity and identity. Form and content are mentioned, but no effort is made to define these expressions. The rules of logic are claimed to be the result of repetition and yet they are said to originate in abstraction. A so-called 'dialectical' logic is set up against formal logic; it is constantly mentioned, but it contains *not one single* rule which would allow us to draw deductions.

In epistemology there is confusion between the problem of the nature of cognition and that of the relations between body and soul. Cognition is explained as being 'a copying, a photographing' of the object; at the same time it is realized that we perceive not these 'photographs' but reality. These 'photographs' are also supposed to 'resemble' light waves. The dialectical materialists *do not deal with one single* argument of the idealists, not even with the famous 'principle of consciousness' – which, incidentally, could be refuted so easily. To refute Kant, they repeat Engels' nonsense. Kant himself could assume – and with full justification – that we are capable of producing alizarine and of discovering new planets; these facts cannot possibly have any connection with his 'thing-in-itself' which, after all, is external to the empirical universe. The problem of the universals is not even broached; it is claimed that everything is subject to change, but that 'eternal laws' operate in the process of change.

In ontology something like the Aristotelian theory of substance ('matter') is taught, but there is not a trace of a philosophical elaboration of this doctrine. The constantly repeated word 'matter' seems devoid of any meaning: for this matter is supposed to have both bodily and spiritual manifestations and, therefore, to be something different from the two – but we are never told what this is. A radically materialistic (therefore categorial-monistic) conception of being is combined with a categorial pluralism. Becoming *(das Werden)* is explained in words which seem to be completely devoid of sense. More particularly, Dialectical Materialism does not seem to notice that the process of becoming is actually a process of *becoming,* the actualization of something and not only annihilation. The dialectical leap is supposed to be 'sudden', yet it is supposed sometimes to last a long time, at any rate to take some time.

In the field of psychology the position of materialism is never properly cleared up: we are not told whether it is epiphenomenal, actiological or functional materialism. The assertion is made that spirit exists but the fact is glossed over that its dependence on the body presents difficult problems. The problem of free will is completely ignored: what Dialectical Materialism calls 'freedom' is nothing but man's ability to apprehend and make use of the laws of nature.

But the situation of axiology is worst of all. Dialectical Materialism demands a heroic attitude and makes moral judgments galore. But the theory of Dialectical Materialism has nothing to say about them. *Not a single* question of theoretical ethics is submitted to detailed discussion. In aesthetics we find an extreme utilitarianism which, incidentally, has not been given a sound philosophical foundation.

What is more, a great deal in this philosophy is quite simply devoid of all sense; for instance, the word 'dialectic' – which is used constantly. The general is 'dialectically' associated with the particular; absolute truth is made to result 'dialectically' from the sum of relative truths; red is made to resemble light waves 'dialectically', and so forth.

A person who has not concerned himself with philosophy may not realize immediately what all this means. But any Western philosopher of whatever complexion will see in these nothing but monstrosities.

We want to emphasize once again that we are not concerned here with the correctness of the views propounded by Dialectical Materialism. Many of its views are, as we have said, correct in our opinion; for the rest, *everything* that is stated by it is also maintained by other philosophies. The point is that it is quite impossible for Western European philosophy to make statements *in the way* Dialectical Materialism makes them. In the Western European sense of the word Dialectical Materialism is not a scientific philosophy.

5. THE FUNDAMENTAL VIEWS. But perhaps it might be found that Dialectical Materialism, despite the primitive character, nay, the senselessness of its analyses and formulations is, at any rate in its fundamental views, a coherent doctrine, a conception of the world which might satisfy the theoretical needs of the human mind. For it is quite possible for a basically correct and consistent doctrine to be expressed in a primitive way. In fact there are many who believe that they have here what is substantially a strictly logical system. But analysis shows that this is not the case; not only is Dialectical Materialism primitive in its technical elaborations, but in its basic views and fundamental theses it is by no means free of contradictions. Here are three points in which its inner contradictions are clearly apparent.

1] First of all, it is flagrantly inconsistent to link objectivist and absolutist realism with radical social pragmatism. Nevertheless, Communist philosophy espouses both doctrines: realism in Dialectical Materialism and pragmatism in Historical Materialism. Admittedly a subjective explanation for this inconsistency does exist. Materialism sees in cognition a copy of the object and is, by this token, realistic and objectivist; at the same time it sees in it a reflex of the body and is therefore, of necessity, pragmatic; truth is no longer that which corresponds to transcendental reality but that which reflects the variable conditions of the subject and which corresponds to his vital needs. But, it is one thing to explain the origin of a contradiction and quite another to resolve it. And this contradiction has not been resolved.

2] Dialectical Materialism, in the narrower sense of the word, also contains an inner contradiction. The fact is that in it are linked together scientific materialism and Hegelianism: on the one hand, the dialectical materialists follow Hegel and speak of the multiplicity of phases of being and, on the other, they repeat the thesis of the materialists when they declare that matter – whose essential feature is movement in space – is the only reality. As has been said already, the formulation of this materialism does not make sense; and the basic views from which the inadequate formulations stem are quite obviously contradictory.

3] A similar situation obtains when the problems of man and values are examined. As scientific materialists, the Communists are thorough-going determinists, whatever they themselves may say about it; they do not admit either chance or free will and they reject everything that is not a function of matter. But as they are Hegelians and Marxists as well, they proclaim, in the same breath, the liberation of mankind, the duty to carry out a revolution and they lay stress on the tremendous importance of human will; in other words, in spite of their materialism and of determinism they attach the greatest importance to spiritual values and to freedom. Once again the formulation reveals itself as pure nonsense. Indeed, Hegel's definition of freedom as "awareness of necessity" does mean something as this necessity is of a spiritual nature; with the dialectical materialists, however, this definition loses all meaning as they understand by necessity that imposed by the laws of matter. At the base of this nonsense lies a contradiction pure and simple: the dialectical materialists would like to have a conception of the world which would be purely materialistic and devoid of all values and which, at the same time, would be romantic, moral and Hegelian – and the two are mutually exclusive. We have here, therefore, a conglomeration of contradictory notions which can never be elucidated by any form of criticism worthy of the name.

Behind all these contradictions there is, quite obviously, the unrealizable linking of Hegelianism and materialism. This, in its turn, shows up yet another characteristic of the system: fundamentally it is nothing but an unsuccessful attempt to take the basic dogmas of nineteenth century thought – with all the inconsistencies, the exaggerated romanticism, the evolutionism and monism – and to give them a uniform formulation, establishing them dogmatically as eternal truth. From this point of view Dialectical Materialism reveals itself as a reactionary doctrine which seeks to maintain thought at the level which it has long since passed. In our opinion, such an attempt is contrary to the trend of the philosophic development of the past fifty years and more. Furthermore it represents a retrogression to a period when philosophy was indubitably at its worst. The reader will now understand why we have not felt compelled to submit to philosophic criticism the content of Dialectical Materialism; indeed, philosophic criticism cannot possibly find a subject for study in this jumble of truisms and borrowings from positivism and Hegelianism which violently contradict one another. We repeat, once again, that we categorically reject not only various theses which have been presented here, but also the basic attitude which implies an attempt to return to the nineteenth century. We are sure that all of this doctrine can be criticized efficaciously and demolished by analysis; but, it is far wiser to do this by reference to Western European systems which contain all that is taught by Dialectical Materialism, but far more efficiently worked out and formulated.

6. RESORT TO THE SOCIOLOGICAL POINT OF VIEW AND ITS LIMITA-TIONS. We have tried to show in the historical section of this book that present-day Russian Dialectical Materialism is a product of Russian civilization. What was said subsequently about its spirit has demonstrated that this actually is so; for this spirit is completely different from the spirit of Western European philosophy. Further evidence has been provided by our critical observations made from the standpoint of Western philosophy. It can therefore be stated categorically that we here deal with a product of an utterly alien civilization. This, in our opinion, is the most significant result of our study.

But if that is so, then the question arises whether a critical study from the point of view of *our* philosophy is appropriate for such a phenomenon? Do we not in our study give absolute validity to our views and points of view? Ought we not rather consider Dialectical Materialism as an alien, exotic and interesting phenomenon without attempting to judge it? An affirmative answer is given to this last question by, for instance, the scholars grouped around *Soviet Studies*. They maintain that one should, so to speak, "raise oneself to the sociological standpoint", i.e., recognize the relativity of every human attitude, and that one should restrict oneself to a purely descriptive survey of the Russian phenomena, philosophy included, without judging them.

Two completely different points of view can be distinguished here. It is self-evident that one should *first* seek to understand every doctrine, however strange it might seem to one; and one cannot understand it if one disregards the connections between it and the social character of the group in which it originated. In this sense the men around *Soviet Studies* are perfectly right and we have endeavoured, just like them, to interpret the phenomenon of Dialectical Materialism against the background of the social conditions and the culture of Russia. In such an interpretation it is obvious that judgments should be limited to questions of fact, not to questions of value. This much seems to be perfectly unequivocal to us.

However, even within the limits of such a purely sociological study which does not seek to pass judgment, one comes across problems which compel one to adopt a critical attitude. For it is just the Russian dialectical materialists and their followers in the West who attribute absolute validity to their point of view. They teach that Russian Dialectical Materialism is the only scientific philosophy. What is more, they claim that it is scientific in the Western European sense of the word, i.e. that it is adapted to the conditions obtaining in Western culture. This claim must be examined; we must find out whether it is justified. This is what we have done, and we have come to the conclusion that this is not the case; Dialectical Materialism does not satisfy the rules of the game obtaining in Western European science; it evidently does not belong to this culture.

So far we have not departed from the sociological standpoint: we merely ascertain facts; for instance, that Dialectical Materialism does not apply the Western European rules for scientific investigation. In our opinion, the sociological standpoint is not a satisfactory point of departure for the philosopher. In a sense the philosopher cannot help doing what the sociologist fears so much: he must of necessity adopt a standpoint to which he attributes an absolute value. No philosopher has been able to escape this requirement and, in fact, even our sociologists do not escape it.

First of all, even sociologists find it necessary to compare among themselves the products of various cultures; whence a certain order arises of its own accord. If it is ascertained that in philosophy *A* several problems are treated in greater detail, more systematically etc., than in philosophy *B*, this is purely a statement of fact. Secondly, there exist certain principles, at any rate in philosophy, which, though worked out in our culture, yet have universal human validity; for instance, the principle that a system must not contain internal contradictions. Finally, some methodological principles have universal validity; they, too, first became apparent to the Greeks but they form part of the general human heritage.

Among these is the principle which states that in philosophy only the results of experience and of logic should be considered, not wishes or anything of that kind.

Here, therefore, are to be found the limits of sociological relativity for the philosopher. He will recognize the system as being the product of a different culture; but having done so, and having investigated the social circumstances in which it originated, he will have to pass judgment on it on the basis of principles which have absolute and universal validity.

7. SUMMARY OF THE RESULTS. The results of our critical observations can be summarized in the following three theses:

1] Present-day Soviet Russian Dialectical Materialism, although it stems also from Western European sources, is, in its essential features, the product of a culture which is alien to the Western European. It is a mistaken notion to acknowledge it as a system of philosophy in the Western European sense of the word.

2] Compared to cognate Western European systems, this materialism is, it is quite obvious, poorer in content and incomparably more primitive in form.

3] It contravenes the conventional rules of philosophic investigation valid in Western Europe* as well as such principles, regarding matter and method, which cannot but be regarded as objectively binding and applicable to all mankind.

And so our final judgment is that it is culturally alien, primitive and substantially false.

XII. CONCLUDING REMARKS

1. THE SUCCESS OF DIALECTICAL MATERIALISM. Why then has Dialectical Materialism in spite of all this, enjoyed such great success with both the masses and numerous intellectuals? If we examine this question from various angles we shall see the answer.

a) First of all, there is no doubt that the moral content of Communism, its campaign for "the liberation of the exploited classes", has gained for it many supporters. These are generally not familiar with Dialectical Materialism and do not realize that this is *not* primarily a social doctrine, but a speculative conception of the world in which the applications to the life of society are rather remote off-shoots. They do not realize that this so-called 'liberation' is by no means the final goal and that the real task is to draw society into unending revolution; more particularly, that this liberation is not intended for the individual man, but for mankind in general. According to the principles of Dialectical Materialism, the individual is always sacrificed to the grandiose dialectical plan as has actually happened in all the states which are under Communist rule. They only see this moral, revolutionary content which, in fact, exerts a great attraction. Consequently, Dialectical Materialism is accepted as the doctrine of the Party which, in its turn, is regarded as the party of liberation.

b) Perhaps there can be perceived behind all this a reaction to the changes which have occurred in our Western European social order. Modern

---

* It would be superfluous to stress the fact that a negative judgment would also be passed on Dialectical Materialism if it were examined in the light of the rules applied by Western science. For what we have said about the spirit of this doctrine (Chapter IV) and about its applications (Chapter IX) makes it absolutely clear that both the theoretical theses of Dialectical Materialism and its practice are incompatible with the scientific rules of research – as research is understood in the West.

society actually does aim at repressing individual liberties and at sub-
stituting, for its centuries-old organic structure, something very like the
structure of Russian society as we have depicted it. For this, Dialectical
Materialism, with its abstract, despotic, communistic character is perfectly adapted. Without doubt an important rôle is played here by an
admiration for the mysterious strangeness and for the true or presumed
power of Russia; but, deeper social motives are probably more important;
the great structural changes in Western Europe seem to have given the
West European mentality a tendency more akin to that of the Russians –
and Dialectical Materialism is, after all, a form of Russian thought.

c) Yet another change seems to have contributed to its success. During
the last century, Europe had come very close to total scepticism; it was on
the point of losing all faith. Now, in the long run, scepticism cannot provide a philosophy of life for a nation because it kills all culture. Today, in
the philosophical thought in Europe, we see clearly a reaction against it.
Dialectical Materialism takes up a radically anti-sceptical position,
practices a veritable cult of philosophy, asserts its eternal validity and
offers a dogmatic faith with binding dogmas. No wonder, then, that many
people who have lost all faith feel themselves reviving in this atmosphere
of Dialectical Materialism and eagerly grasp it as a deliverance from
scepticism.

d) A further reason for its success is to be found in the fact (already
mentioned above) that Dialectical Materialism contains a number of
forgotten truths, which have been despised by many Western philosophers, without which a sensible conception of the world is impossible
and which the world needs. These truths are expressed badly, they often
lose their sense when formulated by dialectical materialists and they contradict the other tenets of this doctrine; but, the fact remains that they are
common-sense truths which are indispensable for life. The ordinary
man – and here the uneducated man and the scholar untrained in philosophy are in the same boat – knows nothing about the technical apparatus
of philosophy. He is incapable of grasping any of its deep problems. The
great strength of Dialectical Materialism lies precisely in the fact that it
advocates, in an unphilosophical manner, the truths of plain common sense
and does not come to grips with the actual problems.

e) One must not overlook the fact that this doctrine exercises a great
power of attraction through yet another element; its romantic conception

of the world and mankind as derived from Hegelianism. This finds expression in the Promethean conception: man, standing alone in a hostile world without God, must rely on his own resources to comprehend and fashion everything; he has been summoned to perform a heroic task which has neither end nor goal; it is his vocation to put into effect an eternal revolution in which he himself, mankind, the earth and the whole universe are involved; a process in which everything is being transformed unceasingly by the power of human will. This, obviously, is not a philosophy; it is a universal atheistic religion proclaimed as if by prophets. It is this religion which attracts so many educated young men in certain countries of the West to Communism.

2. DIALECTICAL MATERIALISM AND CHRISTIANITY. At this point it is quite natural to consider the relationship between Dialectical Materialism and Christianity. In this connection we often come across misunderstandings which can be traced back to two errors in the interpretation of Bolshevik doctrine. Indeed, many people think that we have here a doctrine which resembles the Christian social doctrine; others err in the interpretation of the word 'humanism', believing that they can find, in humanism as understood by Dialectical Materialism, something which corresponds to the deepest demands of Christianity.

It is, of course, quite true that the socialist movement was inspired by ideals of Christian origin; and it is also very possible that *individuals*, professing Dialectical Materialism, revere these ideals. But the *doctrine* itself has, so to speak, nothing to do with them; not only is it in its very essence not a social doctrine – this we have said already – but there is in fact no room in it for anything like the Christian attitude. Humanism, in the form given it by Dialectical Materialism, rejects everything transcendental and all rights of man; what passes for humanism is nothing but belief in the inevitable transformation of human nature and of the world by mankind itself. In other words, this 'humanism' has no points of contact with Christianity.

An even more serious view is to be taken of the fact that the fundamental tenets of Russian Dialectical Materialism are diametrically opposed to those of Christianity. At the focal point of this doctrine is to be found the denial of the existence of God; the dignity of the person is rejected with equal energy for it is conceived as being nothing but a product and a function of society; it is an indisputable fact that everything which transcends matter is negated – however vague the formulation; immortality of the soul is denied; absolute moral values are denied; religion itself – even atheistic religion in Lunačarskij's interpretation – is condemned as an instrument of exploitation and as a myth. This should suffice to show up the incompatibility of the two attitudes.

It has been sometimes said, in this connection, that there can be no clash between Dialectical Materialism and Christianity because the former contains, exclusively, statements of fact whereas the latter concerns itself only with values. This claim is quite obviously false; in fact, it is doubly false. For one thing, it is not true that Dialectical Materialism consists entirely of statements of fact; on the contrary, it contains quite a number of judgments of value and it is inspired by a markedly moralizing spirit. On the other hand, it is not correct to say that Christianity consists only of judgments of value; both theology and anthropology are essential aspects of the Christian faith and both contain statements of fact. The attempt to reconcile, in this manner, the two conceptions of life is therefore based on a misinterpretation of both Dialectical Materialism and of Christianity. However, the opposition can be understood in an even deeper way. Lenin read Ilyin's *Hegel's Philosophy as a Contemplative Theology* with admiration and appreciation. Dialectical Materialism is an interpretation of Hegelianism which is very akin to Ilyin's: it is a divine doctrine which attributes 'truth', i.e., real being and absolute value, to the absolute, to the whole alone. This is sufficiently evidenced by the dogmatic character of this doctrine, by its metaphysical and ethical basic principles, by the attitude of the believing Communists towards the Party. From the Christian point of view, this god is false as are all the deductions which are drawn from this theology and applied to man.

For the Christian, two consequences arise from this: in spite of its primitiveness as a philosophy, Dialectical Materialism is a spiritual current which must not be underestimated; as a movement and as a faith, it has a capacity for the most appalling destruction.

Therefore, it is impossible for Christians and dialectical materialists, as such, to come to terms; each professes a faith which excludes the other. Dialectical Materialism is for Christianity an opponent whose fundamental aim is the total annihilation of Christianity. In view of all this, the Christian 'fellow travellers' are, it would seem, men who have lost their way and who, fundamentally, understand nothing about these problems.

3. DIALECTICAL MATERIALISM AND THE PHILOSOPHERS. The relations between *philosophy* and Dialectical Materialism were discussed in the preceding chapter but a few words must still be said about the problem of the relations between the *philosophers* and the representatives of the Soviet Russian materialism.

First of all, we must expressly state that there are today some men in Russia who, to all appearances, are trying to develop a philosophical attitude; they are making an attempt to work in a manner not unlike ours. We need but refer to Markov's article, which we have discussed, to that part of Kedrov's article which criticizes the one-sidedness of nationalism, to the Soviet psychologists' researches which are frequently very interesting, to Asmus' heroic attitude and to the courageous fight put up by the Soviet logicians in 1950–1951. The fact that such men exist in present-day Russia is a weighty proof for our assertion that there are principles in philosophy which are valid for humanity in general and which transcend the limits of any particular culture. A philosopher would be glad to collaborate with such men, to question them on their thoughts and researches and to discuss problems with them.

But it is a tragic fact that so far these men have been only a minority in Russia; moreover, this minority is being barbarously and systematically attacked and liquidated. Taken as a whole, Soviet Russian Dialectical Materialism adopts an attitude different from theirs. These are its representatives: Mitin, the court philosopher who is always prepared to denounce others, the crude Maksimov, and others like them who alone need be taken seriously; they are the ones who have remained true to the spirit of Lenin's teaching and with whom Western European philosophers come mostly in contact. The representatives of Dialectical Materialism who visit the West from countries under Soviet 'influence' are even less qualified as philosophers. The same applies to those dialectical materialists in the West who are loyal members of the Party, for this Party is, as is well known, directed from Moscow.

So far as these men are concerned, this is what can be said of them: 1] they propound no original ideas but are exponents and propagandists of the official Soviet faith; 2] they specifically profess Lenin's doctrine – according to which, that is "ethical and moral which contributes to the destruction of the old world"; 3] they openly proclaim that they do not seek truth but endeavour to spread propaganda; 4] finally, they scarcely ever use any but offensive terms when speaking of Western European philosophers.

It is, therefore, obvious that Western European thinkers cannot be interested in collaborating with such men; they are not honest philosophers (seekers after truth) but agents of the Communist Party; their aim is to prepare the ground for the Party's use of force – and this leads to the destruction of philosophical life.

APPENDIX I

I. SAMPLES OF RECANTATIONS

1] G. F. Aleksandrov *(Diskussija po knige..., p. 288 et seq.; concluding observations in the discussion of his book): Comrade Ždanov and the other comrades, who have spoken, have pointed out a number of gross *(krupnejšie)* mistakes, errors and imperfections in my book *The History of Western European Philosophy* ... I do not want to conceal from the comrades the fact that I – and, apparently, not I alone – have undergone a rigorous examination in Marxist-Leninist philosophy which, I must admit, we needed as much as we need sunshine and air... This discussion would not have taken place, had not the Central Committee and Comrade Stalin taken us in hand, and it is impossible to say where this crisis would have led if they hadn't. Whatever I myself may feel as the author of this thoroughly unsatisfactory book which has shown me up as a bad *(ploxim)* scholar, yet I find some consolation in the fact that our philosophic workers have rapidly followed comrade Ždanov's directives with regard to the unsatisfactory nature of my book and its philosophical imperfections...

Comrade Ždanov! Comrade Secretary of the Central Committee! The Party has educated and instructed us. We want to be worthy of our Party which has entrusted such great tasks to us. I believe that I express the thought of all the comrades here present when I say: we want to assure the Party through you, Comrade Ždanov, and we give to our beloved Comrade Stalin our firm and honest word as Bolsheviks that we, as a team, are resolved to apply all our passionate enthusiasm to the task of raising the level of philosophical work in our country and of spreading, far and wide, propaganda for Marxism-Leninism. (Short summing-up by A. A. Ždanov: loud applause and cries: Long live Comrade Stalin! Hurrah!)

2] Ju.- Ždanov *(Pravda* of August 7 1948, quoted by *Europe* 26, 1948, No. 33/34, p. 171–173; letter addressed to the Central Committee and to Stalin)*: ... there is no doubt that I have made a number of mistakes.

* Juri Ždanov had only recently become associated with the Central Committee of the Party. In the famous controversy on biology (see *O položenii ...; l'Etat)* he had stated

123

(*1*) ... when it was suggested that I should lecture in the *Seminar* I did not hesitate to develop my own thoughts, having first warned the listeners that I was expressing only my own personal views, so that none of them should think that they were binding. This was undoubtedly the conduct of a 'professor' in the bad sense of the word, not that of a Party member.

(*2*) My fundamental mistake lay in the fact that I tried to mitigate the conflict between the opposing tendencies in biology...

(*3*) It was a mistake on my part to criticize academician Lysenko brutally and in public...

(*4*) Lenin has frequently said that those who assume that this or that phenomenon is inevitable run the risk of falling into objectivism *(ob'-ektivizm)*. This is, to some extent, the error into which I fell. Like another Pimen* I described Weissmanism and Morganism – I draw no distinction between them – as matters of indifference to us, as neither good nor bad. Instead of rejecting these unscientific views (held in our country by Šmalgauzen and his school) which are clericalism in disguise, i.e., theological conceptions,... I committed the mistake of trying to 'take cognizance' of the position of this doctrine in the evolution of biology and of trying to find a 'rational germ' in it. That is why my criticism of Weissmanism was weak, 'objective' and therefore shallow... Such are my errors as I see them... All this because of immaturity and inexperience. I shall correct my errors by my actions.

3] P. M. Žukovskij *(O položenii..., p.* 523 et seq.)**
Comrades! Late last night I made up my mind to make this declaration. I say: late last night, because at that time I did not know then that a letter from Comrade Ju. Ždanov would appear in today's *Pravda*; there is,

---

his views, trying to find a middle course between Lysenko and his victims. The letter is dated July 10 1948, but was published only on the last day of the discussions when it was clear that the authorities gave unequivocal support to Lysenko. – English translation in *Soviet Studies* 1, 1949, p. 175–177.
* Character in Pushkin's *Boris Godunov*.
** During the 'discussion' between Lysenko and the 'Mendelians' on August 5th, 1948, (O položenii..., –. 383–393) Žukovskij had made a long speech in which he tried, like Ju. Ždanov, to maintain a position between the antagonists. S. I. Alixanjan (p. 525 et seq.) and I. M. Poljakov (p. 526 et seq.) made similar recantations.

therefore, no connection between this declaration of mine and Comrade Ju. Ždanov's letter. I believe the Deputy Minister of Agriculture, Lobanov, can testify to the fact that I telephoned to him yesterday asking for permission to make this declaration today ... I am referring to my injudicious speech of two days ago *(O položenii...*, p. 383–393); as is stated here, it was the last time I took up position against Mičurin although previously I had never personally opposed his doctrine. But, in fact it was the last time that I took up a position supported by incorrect *(nepravilnyx)* biological and ideological ideas ... Bear witness to the fact that today I perform a 'Party-act' and show myself a true member of the Party, i. e. prove myself to be honest *(čestno)*.

4] B. M. Kedrov *(Kultura i Žizn'*, 22. III. 1949, quoted by *Soviet Studies* I, 1949 (1), p. 85 et seq.)*:
I consider it my duty as a Party member to declare that I fully agree with this criticism (of M. Mitin) and that I categorically condemn the hostile cosmopolitanism which I have stood for in the past... My error arose from the fact that I distorted Lenin's principle of partisanship and strayed in the direction of bourgeois objectivism and apolitism. I fully admit that the observations made by Comrade A.A. Ždanov during the philosophical discussion are unquestionably applicable to me when he says that the philosophical errors of many philosophers stem from "insufficient knowledge of the fundamental principles of Marxism-Leninism and from survivals of bourgeois ideology". It was a grave error on my part not to have immediately obeyed the Party's criticism and not to have immediately abandoned my erroneous opinions.

2. DESCRIPTION OF SOME PHILOSOPHERS

(According to Judin-Rozental': of course, further explanations can be found in this text and, even more so, in more comprehensive books; however, the following quotations – all of them taken from the 'classics' – are common property of Russian Dialectical Materialism).
Aristotle: Great thinker of the ancient world, scholar of genius...,

---

* See Chapter III for details of the conflict.

vacillates between idealism and materialism... Approaches materialism in his epistemology (16; 29 et seq.).*

Descartes: "(In philosophy) D. was an idealist" (55a; 128a).

Kant: "The essential doctrine of Kantian philosophy is an amalgam of materialism and idealism, a compromise between the two" (98a; 217a). "This philosophy was the ideology of the young German bourgeoisie which needed a critique of the philosophical and juridical notions of the feudal era" (99a). "Natural rubber was a 'thing in itself' for as long as chemistry had not succeeded in producing it" (30b; 75a).

Locke: "Materialist" (135b; 295a).

Neo-Kantianism: "The most important among the bourgeois philosophical tendencies of the second half of the nineteenth century which adapted the content of Kant's philosophy and fitted it, with some elaborations, into increasingly sterile, reactionary, lifeless, subjectively idealistic systems" (190; 399a).

Plato: "Ancient philosopher, idealist, champion of a slave-owning aristocracy' (213a; in the fourth edition 'slave-owning' has been replaced by 'reactionary' 460 et seq.).

Positivism: "One of the most widespread idealistic tendencies of bourgeois philosophy" (215a; 464a).

Pragmatism: "Reactionary, idealistic tendency" (217a; fourth edition: 'subjectively idealistic', 474a).

Stalin: "Thinker of genius and leader of the world proletariat, Lenin's great collaborator and comrade, who has carried on Marx', Engels' and Lenin's doctrine and tasks" (295a). The fourth edition says merely: "Faithful disciple and close collaborator of Lenin, who ... (etc. as above), (567b). (In his *On Dialectical and Historical Materialism*) (Stalin) raises Dialectical Materialism onto a new, a higher plane". (265a).

3. THE PRINCIPLE OF CONTRADICTION AND LOGISTICS

Certain dialectical materialists are in the habit of appealing to logistics when seeking to justify the position they adopt in relation to the principle

* The first number refers to the second edition (1940), the second to the fourth edition (1954).

of contradiction; logistics, they claim, would admit the denial of this principle. Here is what we have to say on the subject:

1] In logistics a distinction must be drawn between logic and meta-logic and in logic itself between 'classical' logic and the 'heterodox' systems.

2] Now, metalogic has been, so far at any rate, consistently two-valued and free of contradiction; we know no metalogic other than the two-valued one. This is important because metalogic corresponds just to that which is considered 'logic' by those who do not practise logistics: it is a system of rules which permit deductions to be drawn, while the so-called logic in logistics is strictly formal, therefore devoid of significant content and not enabling one to make deductions.

3] In 'classical' logistics (as it is to be found in *Principia Mathematica* and in Leśniewski) the principle of contradiction has as much validity – if not more – as in traditional logic. For this logistic always contains propositions and rules which make it possible to deduce any desired proposition from a contradiction; this removes the distinction between acknowledged and not acknowledged propositions and consequently the distinction between true and false propositions, and leads to a complete surrender of knowledge. That is why it is customary in logistics to examine systems very carefully to see whether or not they contain contradictions; for this purpose complicated and exact methods have been devised.

4] Among the 'heterodox' systems of logic there are several which do not contain the principle of the excluded middle (intuitive systems); there is one (Kolmogorov's system) which makes it possible, on the basis of a contradiction, not to prove any given proposition but to prove the nega-tion of any given proposition; but there is a whole group of systems, the many-valued systems of logic, which do not admit the principle of contra-diction and which cannot prove any of the above-mentioned sceptical deductions. Now the *logical* character of these systems is a doubtful quantity; some of the terms which occur in them are apparently quite incapable of logical interpretation and the specialists in logistics, who at one time were enthusiastic supporters of such systems, are now, in the majority, very sceptical of them.

And so, on the whole, logistical investigation has not 'overcome' Aris-totle's assertion that denial of the principle of contradiction leads to

scepticism and to surrender of knowledge; on the contrary, it has considerably strengthened this assertion, having provided rigorous technical
evidence for proving its theses.

APPENDIX II*)

I. SUPPLEMENTS

to page 19: The Three Periods of Modern Thought
in Western Europe

The thought of Western Europe has passed through three periods since the end of the Middle Ages (more precisely, since the late Renaissance). The first period, from the late Renaissance to the eighteenth century, is characterized by the deification of the secular – the severing of philosophy, science, politics, art, etc. from the transcendent and sacred. In the 18th century, however, took place a movement in a, to some extent, opposite direction – the secular, freed from the transcendent, was now deified. History, mankind, progress, even the universe was considered and felt to be *holy*. The speculative apex of this movement is in the philosophy of Hegel, but it is as well evident in the materialism, evolutionism and other trends of the nineteenth century. Finally, with the commencement of the twentieth century (with significant predeccessors such as Kierkegaard and Nietzsche already in the nineteenth century) begins a new trend – the secular was desanctified – thus a philosopher of the twentieth century can say: "the question as to whether there is a progressive evolution or not has no meaning for me because *I* must die". For the comprehension of Diamat it is absolutely essential to realize that it rises *entirely* from the *second* period.

to page 22: The Younger Marx and Diamat

Among researchers it is a universally recognized fact that Marx underwent a development in which at least two phases can be distinguished, the 'younger' and the 'older' Marx. The earlier period is marked by an attitude which is humanistic in the strict sense of the term – the individual stands in the centre of Marx' thought and Marx, himself, is a convinced democrat. What is even of more importance is that it seems that the younger Marx, under the influence of Feuerbach, in a certain sense belongs to the pre-

* In this section the numbers in parentheses (not preceded by a letter) refer to the position in the *Bibliographie der sowjetischen Philosophie* (by Blakeley, etc.).

decessors of the third period of modern, Western thought insofar as he protested against Hegel's 'Totality' *(Ganze)* and put the emphasis on the real, concrete man (and on the real-concrete in general). It was in this same period that Marx developed his significant doctrine on alienation. Later we find not a rejection of these elements but, rather, a shift in emphasis. The humanistic is adjourned to a mythical future; the present is ruled by a theory of the means which are necessary for realizing the 'paradise on earth', and these means are conceived in a completely Hegelian spirit. The thought on the concrete also received a reinterpretation so that in the centre, instead of the really human individual, we find a 'scientific' reality – i.e. a basically abstract world and society. This 'later' Marx was further developed by Engels. In Soviet-Russian Diamat there are very few traces of the thought of the 'younger' Marx. Thus, for example, I found the word 'alienation' (i.e. the corresponding Russian word, *otčuždenie)* in the relevant literature, for the first time in 1958 – and, even then it was in quotation marks as a foreign word used in a polemic against Calvez who had interpreted Marx precisely from the point of view of alienation. For this very reason it is erroneous to identify the Soviet Diamat with 'Marxism'. The thoughts of the early Marx have absolutely *no* significance for the content of Diamat – they serve only as means whereby the Party gains supporters among the Western intellectuals who are not under Russian power.

to page 28: Toward a Socio-Economic Interpretation
of Diamat's History

The phenomena described above can be interpreted, at least partially, from the standpoint of the Marxian doctrine of the dependence of thought on the 'base'. For, we find in the Russia of the end of the nineteenth century socio-economic relations which are very different from those of the Germany or England of around 1850. Then, too, the spiritual context in which Russian thought developed is, as has been said, conditioned by a very different history. As a result, in order that it might find a hearing in Russia, the thought of Marx (or, better, of Engels) had to be reinterpreted and supplemented in a way which seems strange and even senseless from the standpoint of the West. This does not mean that these thoughts of Engels were not accepted; they were accepted – only from them resulted something very different from what is found elsewhere.

In the same line of thought, it seems valid to conjecture that contemporary Soviet thought (since 1945) must be different from that of the old Russian intelligentsia and from that of Lenin. For, between 1917 and 1945 the 'base' in the Soviet Union was transformed – we now find there at least to some extent, a highly industrialized civilization. As a matter of fact, there are signs of tendencies which are completely different from those described here, whereas they approximate certain trends which we find, for example, in the USA.

to page 64: The Structure of Dialectical Materialism According to
the *Osnovy marksistskoj filosofii* of 1958

In the Autumn of 1958 a change, although not essential, in the Stalinist scheme was for the first time officially introduced by the Academy of Sciences of the Soviet Union in a textbook entitled, *Osnovy marksistskoj filosofii* (Principles of Marxist Philosophy). The external division into 'dialectic' and 'materialism' is dropped but, as a matter of fact, it reappears insofar as materialism is treated in Chapters 4 and 5, and the 'dialectic' is the subject of Chapters 6 to 10. Significant is the fact that – in accordance with my criticism published in earlier editions of the present work – 'materialism' is now put at the beginning. In the place of Stalin's four 'laws' we find only three in formal presentation; nevertheless, the first law (that of 'inter-connection') appears as a sort of introduction to Chapter 6. The three new laws are: 1] the law of the "transition from a quantitative to a qualitative change" (Ch. 7), 2] "the unity and battle of contradictions" (Ch. 8), 3] "the negation of negation" (Ch. 9). Therefore, the entire content of the Stalinist 'dialectic' is taken with the addition of the law of "the negation of negation" (which is originally from Engels and had been omitted by Stalin). This new 'law' reads: "the dialectical negation is the basis of a development which assumes and preserves within itself all that is positive in the preceding stage ... and (a development) which has, on the whole, a progressive character" (p. 301). It contains, then, the notion of necessary progress (which was also present in Stalin's treatment), but, further, we find the addition of the Hegelian doctrine of synthesis (see p. 91 in the text) which was, in Lenin's version, rather in the background. It is possible that Stalin's omission of this 'law' was no accident.

to page 68 ff.: More Recent Changes in the Situation in the
Single Philosophic Disciplines

The situation of *logic* seems to have improved in the course of the last few years. The Autumn of 1957 saw the opening of a seminar for logic in the Faculty of Philosophy of the University of Moscow; a seminar which, according to reports received, is devoted above all to mathematical logic, and this thanks especially to Prof. S. A. Janovskaja and her school. In 1955/56 took place an acrimonious public debate between two logicians, N. Kondakov and K. S. Bakradze, on the one hand, and the 'reactionaries', on the other – and these first were permitted to publish their arguments in the *VF (VF* 1956, 2*)*. The most striking event, however, was the interventions of a group of mathematical logicians, who opposed the usual (and completely untenable from a scientific point of view) interpretation of the "Law of Contradiction", and who maintained that there can be no contradictions, in the Aristotelian sense of the word, in things *(VF* 1958, 12*)*. The productivity of Soviet logicians (in the strict sense of the word) is, quantitatively and qualitatively, constantly growing.

Psychology has developed further and attained an independent status. For example, there is a section for psychology at the University of Moscow, which has five laboratories or sub-sections. The psychologists have a separate journal *(Voprosy psixologii)* at their disposal and, in addition, many psychological articles are published in pedagogical journals. As far as content is concerned, Soviet psychology remains under the direction of the theses of the 'Pavlovian Conference' (1950). In 1950–1955 there was a long discussion in the *VF* on the interpretation of these theses, in which more spiritualistically and more materialistically inclined psychologists took part. As it stands today, psychic phenomena are identical with the physiological – nevertheless, psychology has its own proper object and its method includes introspection.

Ethics, too, has recently achieved an independent status in Soviet philosophy. In 1951 a programme for a course in this discipline was published (137) and, since that time, a fair number of books on ethics has appeared (see, for example, 1129, 1262, 1268(2), 1199) – these books deal above all with education in Communist morality (see, e.g., 1122, 1149, 1263, 1245, 1025) and with opposition to 'bourgeois' morality (1268(1)). Characteristic, too, is the fact that a very long chapter of the *Osnovy* (pp. 575–582) is devoted to ethics. As regards content, the novelty is the fact that one now speaks of a 'golden base' *(zolotoj fond)* of human nature, and that it is maintained that Communist morality does not reject everything from the past epochs because this very 'golden base' always remains.

We find more literature but little new in *aesthetics*. – Nevertheless, this discipline, too, seems to be slowly winning an independent status.

to page 102: The Empirical Sciences and Diamat

Through the implementation of the Stalinist decision of 1950 and as well through the force of circumstances, the situation of the empirical sciences and, above all, that of physics has improved.

In 1954 G. E. Glezerman distinguished in the empirical sciences (but, not in the social sciences) two elements: the non-partisan single propositions and laws on the one hand, and the general theories which are partisan *(parteigebunden),* on the other. In the official *Osnovy* (1958) we find: "also the general theoretical problems of the empirical sciences are a battlefield of the ideological war, which reflects, in one way or another, the class-war" (p. 373). In practice, however, at least physics has achieved such an independence that now (since 1955) it is accepted that the philosopher is competent not to dictate sentences to this science but only to interpret its results. The situation is less encouraging in the other sciences such as biology and psychology. The vague formulation of the above-quoted dogmatic statement permits the Party to interfere at will, in the name of Diamat.

II. THE ORGANIZATION AND SPIRIT OF CONTEMPORARY SOVIET PHILOSOPHY

1. *More Recent Developments: Chronology*

The development of Soviet philosophy in the recent past is, without a doubt, conditioned by numerous and, to some extent, profound changes in the socio-economic structure of the country. One needs only to bear in mind: that a new generation has grown up since the revolution – a generation which, *first*, is not made up of demagogues, as was true of the old Bolsheviks, but rather of, at least to some extent, highly educated specialists who often possess a good general formation; that, *second*, the intelligentsia which makes up the ruling class in the Soviet Union is more conscious of its social position and its real power; that, *third*, the Soviet Union has developed from a backward land to an industrial state, consequent upon which scientific research experienced a tremendous boom. It is easy to understand why the mechanical repetition of massive slogans – such as are most of the propositions of Stalin's "classical" pamphlet – has become progressively more impossible. A generation of intellectuals who have been educated in universities, in contact with true science, and who are accustomed to working with a highly developed technical apparatus *must* search for a better philosophy. What is more significant is the fact that now they *can* demand it, for nothing can go on without the physicists, such as Bloxincev, who direct the atomic research centres. In general, the ruling powers, i.e., the Party, cannot afford to ignore the new intelligentsia.

So much for the socio-economic presuppositions of the change. These find theoretical expression in, among others, two authoritative doctrines which are universally accepted and which have contributed tremendously to the acceleration of the process. The first is the 1937 theory of non-antagonistic contradictions, attributed to Mao Tse-tung, recognized by Stalin and Ždanov (1947) and then by all in the Soviet Union. The second is Stalin's doctrine (1950) according to which there are *spiritual-social* factors – namely, language – which are not superstructural, hence not to be considered as partisan. We will review these doctrines shortly and indicate their theoretical significance.

The basic thought of Mao Tse-tung which interests us here can be formulated as follows. The so-called 'contradiction' possesses its 'generality', i.e. it is present in all beings, but also has its 'particularity', i.e. in each case it assumes another form. As a matter of fact, this is a logical consequence of two laws of the so-called 'dialectic': i.e. that there are 'contradictions' everywhere and that there are qualitatively different levels of being in the world. From this Mao infers something new; namely, that the 'struggle' of 'contradictions' must be different for each qualitative level. And, he infers further that this struggle must be different in 'socialist' society from what it was in the 'pre-socialist' class-society. While the 'struggle' of 'contradictions' in the latter is 'antagonistic', grows more acute with time and can be removed only by a revolution, in a 'socialist' society it is 'non-antagonistic', is mollified in the course of

134

time, and can be removed by good methods – 'criticism and self-criticism'. This has important consequences for philosophic life. For, once Mao's doctrine is accepted, then the 'struggle', i.e. discussion, can go on even in a 'socialist' society. And, this 'battle' need not be settled by executions and deportations to concentration camps – 'criticism and self-criticism' should suffice. Once accepted, this principle helped Soviet philosophy to come out of its 'quiet', i.e. dead, period.

For all that, of much greater importance was Stalin's 1950 intervention. Against the doctrine of the leading Soviet linguist, Nikolaj Jakovlevič Marr (1864–1934; cfr. 508, p. 265a), Stalin taught that language is not super-structural, is not tied to the economic base (i.e. to the *relations* of produc-tion) hence, is not class-bound. Since language is something, so taught Stalin, which is necessary to production itself, it belongs to the *forces* of production which underlie the base. Therefore, it is common to capitalist and proletariat – it is not class-bound but national.

In these arguments which concern directly language and linguistics one premiss is implicit, namely that everything which is necessary to produc-tion itself is not superstructural, but is above considerations of class. And, there are numerous factors of this type – an obvious one is technology and with it the sciences by which it is conditioned. Once this principle is accepted then it becomes possible to free such factors from a class-bound character and, consequently, from the obligatory party-mindedness. They become the general and objective possessions of all mankind. But, this promises the scientist, and in part the philosopher too, a certain freedom of research. What is not class-bound, is not dependent on Diahistomat – i.e. on the supposedly proletarian theory – and thus is not subject to the decrees of the party-organs.

It is clear that this Stalinist principle has no application in the social sciences, but its significance for the other domains was very great. This made itself felt first of all in logic, but after 1950 even the interpretation of the empirical sciences was able to take on forms which had not previously been admitted.

The following is a chronology of the most important events in Soviet philosophy in the period 1946–1959:

November 1946: *Decree of the Central Committee on the introduction of logic and psychology* as subjects in the middle-schools.

January 1947: Discussion in the Institute of Philosophy on G. F. Aleksandrov's *History of Philosophy*.
16 to 25 June 1947: *Congress* to criticize the above book, including the speech of A. A. Ždanov.
September 1947: First issue of *Voprosy filosofie*.
1947: Logic texts by V. F. Asmus, Vinogradov, etc.

March 1948: M. A. Markov's article on physical knowledge.
23 March 1948: Condemnation by S. V. Kaftanov, Minister of Higher Education, of a-political and formalistic logic.
June 1948: First conference of logic teachers for criticism of V.F. Asmus
July 1948: Logic program of the Ministry of Higher Education.
31 July to 7 August 1948: Conference on the situation in the biological sciences (Lysenko Affair).
1948: First conference on philosophical question of physics (in Charkov).

11 March 1949: Self-criticism of B. M. Kedrov.
Beginning of 1949: B. M. Kedrov no longer editor-in-chief of *VF*; four members of the editorial staff dropped.
8 to 15 July 1949: All-Soviet conference of professors of Marxism-Leninism and philosophy. Speech of S. V. Kaftanov.

9 May 1950: Article on linguistics in "Pravda", by A. S. Čibakova.
20 June 1950: *Stalin's essay on Marxism and linguistics in Pravda* (further in 4 July and 2 August).
28 June to 4 July 1950: *"Pavlovian" Conference*.

1950/51: Discussion on formal logic and the dialectic in *VF* and various institutes.

September 1952: Stalin's *Economic Problems of Socialism in the SU*.
1952: Translation of the *Analytics* of Aristotle.
24 December 1952: M. A. Suslov's attack on the president of the Institute of Philosophy, P. N. Fedoseev *(Izvestija* 12 and 21 December 1952).

18 January 1953: Self-criticism of the Institute of Philosophy in the *VF*.
5 March 1953: Death of Stalin.

10 August 1953: Institute of Philosophy integrated into the Section for Economy and Law of the Academy of Sciences.

January 1954: All-Soviet seminar for teachers of social sciences.
16 March 1954: G. F. Aleksandrov named Minister of Culture under Malenkov.
April 1954: Decision on the discussion on psychology.
23 to 28 August 1954: Philosophic Congress in Zürich; first appearance of Soviet philosophers abroad.

8 February 1955: Downfall of Malenkov and G. F. Aleksandrov (replaced by N. Mixajlov).
March 1955: *Decision in the discussion on philosopic problems of the theory of relativity.* A. A. Maksimov attacked.

14 to 22 February 1956: 20th Party Congress. 'De-Stalinization'.
June 1956: Decree of the Central Committee on the introduction of a course in Diahistomat in all upper schools.
September 1956: Opening of a logic seminar in the Institute of Philosophy

1958: Discussion on contradictions in the Institute of Philosophy.
April 1958: First issue of *Filosofskie nauki.*
12 to 18 September 1958: Numerous Soviet philosophers take part in the 13th Intenational Congress in Venice.
21 to 25 October 1958: All-Soviet conference on philosophic questions of modern natural sciences (in Moscow).
End of 1958: Publication of the collective work, *Principles of Marxist Philosophy.*

2. Centres of Study and Research

There are numerous universities and institutes in the Soviet Union where philosophy is taught and philosophic research carried on. According to statistics published in *Voprosy filosofii* for the years 1947, 1948, 1951, 1951/52 and 1953/54, philosophical theses were submitted for the degree of Candidate of Science at no fewer than 36 such institutions. (*VF* 47, 2, 372f.; 51, 6, 211–217; 53, 1, 230–237; 55, 3, 197–211). Since this degree is

taken at the end of a course of academic study, there must have been regular courses in philosophy at these universities and institutes.*
As far as is known, fourteen of these institutions are in Moscow, 23 in the provinces. In 1947 there were only 6, all in Moscow.
It is interesting to note the progressive decentralization of study and research. The following table clearly illustrates the point.

Number of institutes to which philosophic dissertations
were presented*

Year	1947	1948–1951	1951/2	1953/4	total
Moscow	6	5	11	11	14
Province	0	5	17	19	23
Total	6	10	28	30	37
Moscow in %	100%	50%	39%	36%	38%

Needless to say, these academic centres are not all on the same level, quantitatively or qualitatively. It appears that about 10 % of all philosophy students have attended the University of Moscow. The following details will give an idea of the range of studies at this university.
According to A. P. Gagarin there were 1,150 philosophy students there in the academic year 1950/51. Of these, 489 were registered in the philosophical, 168 in the psychological department, 272 were correspondence students *(zaočnie)* and 69 were day students. In addition, there were 152 aspirants.

* In the Soviet Union a university course lasts 4 to 6 years. The academic year consists of two terms, from September 1 to January 23 and from February 7 to June 30. The student has to take examinations at the end of each year, otherwise he is not allowed to carry on for another year. Two 'unsatisfactory's' entail automatic exclusion. At the end of his course the student takes an examination. Then, if he has received good marks, he can become an 'aspirant'. As such he acts as assistant to a professor and prepares a thesis for the degree of Candidate of Science (in our case 'philosophic science'). This thesis is then submitted after three years probation and must now (since 1957) be printed before it is submitted. The thesis must give evidence of new knowledge and the standard required is that of a doctoral thesis at a Swiss university. (K. G. Gallin, *Vysšee obrazovanie i podgotovka kadrov v SSSR*. Moscow. 1958).
* For this table and those following, Blakeley, *Dissertations* has been extensively used.

As regards the number of teachers, the following details are based on a report by E. D. Klementev and others compiled in 1957 (and referring probably to the academic year 1956/57).

	Professors	Assoc. Prof.	Assistants	Total
Diahistomat	6	5	7	18
History of foreign Phil.	3	6	5	14
History of Phil. of the nations of the SU	3	7	2	12
Total for 3 'kafedry'	12	18	14	44

The psychology section was, if not larger, at any rate as large as the history section. It included five different laboratories or sub-departments. The *kafedra* for logic cannot, in view of the great interest in this subject, have been much smaller than the psychology section. It is, therefore, not unlikely that the corresponding figures for these two departments would, taken together, be 57, of whom 17 were professors.

When one remembers that no fewer than 14 Muscovite institutions gave instruction in philosophy, it will hardly be an exaggeration to put the total number of philosophy teachers at these establishments at about 300 instructors, including about 100 (university) professors.

We also have a few details on the State University in Tiflis *(Tbilisi)*. According to a report by A. A. Gelašvili (228) of 1956 (referring presumably to the year 1955/56) this institution had three departments; Dialectical and Historical Materialism, Logic, History of Philosophy. There were 15 teachers in the first department. Tiflis is a fairly important centre of philosophical research, thanks above all to the work of Prof. K. S. Bakradze, but the other provincial universities are probably not much smaller. It may be assumed that each of them has a teaching staff of about 30.

3. Theses

The lists of philosophical dissertations for the degree of Candidate of Science* throw further light on the extent and distribution of the teaching of philosophy. The following is an over-all statistical view.

	1947	1948–1951	1951/52	1953/54	total
in Moscow	66	225	149	300	740
in the Provinces	0	15	54	169	238
Total	66	240	203	469	978
Annual average	66	80	203	469	163
In comparison with 1947 (= 100)	100	121	308	711	
Share of Muscovite institutions	100%	94%	73%	64%	76%

It is impossible to check whether and how far these figures are complete, but it is highly likely that the increase in the numbers is not only due to an improvement in the access to sources of information. The increasing share of the provinces – rising from 0% to 36% with six years – is probably not merely statistical. The final figure is, in any case, quite significant – 469 theses in the year 1953/54.

Among the institutions at which these were submitted, three, namely the Academy of Social Sciences, the Institute of Philosophy of the Academy of Sciences of the USSR and the University of Moscow, occupy a leading position. At these institutions the following number of theses was submitted:

* The degree of doctor is awarded after the public defence of a thesis. Only a few of the professors of philosophy have this degree. The number of doctorates is relatively small – for example, according to I. D. Andreev and others (18), altogether 14 doctorates in philosophy were awarded in 1953 and the beginning of 1954. The names include: F. V. Konstantinov, F. Ja. Moskalenko, G. V. Platonov, A. V. Savinov, V. I. Selivanov, V. F. Golosov, R. Garaudy, S. M. Kavalev, all of them well-known Soviet philosophers. According to a report by E. V. Šoroxova, eight doctoral theses were defended at the Institute of Philosophy in the first half of 1956.

	1947	1948–51	1951/52	1953/54	total
Acad. of Soc.					
Sciences	32	128	34	52	246
Inst. of Phil.	10	67	25	37	139
U. of Moscow	11	28	60	139	238
Total	53	223	119	228	623
Annual average	53	74	119	228	108
in comparison					
with 1947 (= 100)	100	140	225	430	—

The picture here is essentially similar to that offered by the first table. But, in all probability, the information on the Muscovite institutions comes from sources which are better informed than those which report on the provinces.

These figures enable us to estimate the number of philosophy students in the Soviet Union. In 1950/51 489 persons were studying philosophy in the University of Moscow. If we take away 189 for psychology, there remain about 300 for pure philosophy. In 1951/52 60 theses were submitted at this university, out of a total of 203, i.e. roughly one-third. This suggests that the number of philosophy students in Soviet universities was about 1,000 in that year. In 1953/54 the number of theses more than doubled (from 203 to 469). It will be, therefore, no exaggeration to estimate that at least 2,000 young men and women were training to be philosophers. Naturally, these are only round figures, not precise statistics. All the same, they are remarkable.

4. Publications

In various respects Soviet philosophical publications differ from those of the West. In the first place, they are extremely centralized – only very few institutions publish anything worth mentioning. The editions of the works that are published are much larger than is usual with Western publications of a similar nature. Moreover, there are comparatively few strictly scientific publications while numerous textbooks and writings of a popular character are published. In all these respects, however, there has been some development in the direction of Western conditions: centralization is becoming less intense and editions are becoming smaller. Also, more scientific publications are appearing.

As far as periodicals are concerned, Soviet philosophers had only one professional journal between 1947 and 1957, *Voprosy filosofii*. At the beginning of 1958 a new philosophical journal, *Filosofskie nauki*, was established, which represents the philosophical series in the "Scientific Contributions of the Ministry of Higher Education".

Philosophical articles can also be published in the Academy's *Izvestija* and similar series published by the Academies of Sciences and a few universities, and also in other organs. For example, A. A. Maksimov published one of his notorious denunciations in *Literaturnaja gazeta* and another in the Navy journal. The leading periodicals and newspapers, such as *Kommunist, Pravda,* etc., also publish articles of philosophical importance from time to time.

Nevertheless, the most important journal is still *Voprosy filosofii*. It is the main source for every scholar and student in this field and is now one of the most important philosophical journals in the world. Founded in 1947, two issues were published in that year, three a year between 1948 and 1950, six a year between 1951 and 1956 and since 1957 12 issues a year have appeared. The total number of pages rose from 897 in 1947 to over 2,300 in 1958. The edition of 20,000 copies in the years 1947 and 1948 rose to 50,000 in 1956 and was then limited to 32,500 (presumably in connection with the change-over to monthly publication). During the first ten years (1947–1956) *VF* published more than 1,000 articles and notes by nearly 800 different writers. Quantitatively at any rate, it represents a tremendous achievement, especially when one remembers that one page of this journal corresponds to about 2 1/2 of the octavo pages normally used in the West. If printed in Western style the contents of the ten years' issues would form a small library of about 50 volumes containing 500 pages each.

As far as the contents are concerned, the history of *VF* has often been one of suffering and misfortune. Under the bold and intelligent direction of B. M. Kedrov, it became in 1948 the target of attacks by A. A. Maksimov. After the second number of 1948 (permit of publication given October 27 1948), publication was suspended and the next issue (1948, 3) did not appear until June 1 1949. Kedrov was no longer editor-in-chief, and four members of the editorial staff had been dropped. Maksimov himself became an editor, beginning with the first issue of 1949; before this, a similar reactionary, M. B. Mitin, had been nominated to the post. From 1949 to August 1952 (*VF* 1952, 4) the journal was edited by D. I. Česnokov; then F. V. Konstantinov became editor-in-chief for two years (until *VF* 1955, 4). Maksimov was still a member of the editorial board when the editor made a sharp attack on him (in the first issue of 1955). Some time later (*VF* 1955, 4) he disappeared from the editorial staff.

Apart from the journals, Soviet philosophers also have at their disposal a number of collective works, which appear within the framework of the publications of various universities and also independently. As far as such symposia on philosophy are concerned, the first known to us during the period from 1947 onwards was published by the Academy of Sciences of the Azerbaijan SSR in 1948 (1276). This was followed by *Questions of Philosophy,* published by the Institute of Philosophy of the Academy of Sciences (1310), the *Academic Contributions* of the Academy of Social Sciences attached to the Central Committee (900), both of which appeared in 1950; then came *Problems of Dialectical and Historical Materialism* from the same Academy in 1953 (1307). The year 1955 saw the production of no less than five similar volumes, two of which were published in Leningrad (899, 1075), two in Sverdlovsk (901, 1076) and one in Minsk (1317). Beginning in 1956 publications of this kind have become increasingly numerous.

Bibliographically the situation in Soviet philosophy is unsatisfactory. Current bibliographies were not published in *VF* until 1952. These are indicated in "Sovietica" (see below) by the numbers: 582(29), (31), (35), (38), (47), (50), (54), (55), (56); 2029 (7), (19), (21), (25), (31), (38), (41). According to the *Bibliography of Soviet Philosophy* current bibliographies exist of the publications on philosophy acquired by the library of the Academy of Sciences, but they are only duplicated and hence fairly inaccessible. The work of G. A. Wetter and the essays of H. Dahm in *Ost-Probleme* contain valuable bibliographies. In 1959 there appeared two issues of the *Bibliography of Soviet Philosophy* in the series *Sovietica,* edited by Th. Blakeley and the staff of the Institute of East-European Studies in Fribourg (Switzerland). The first of these contains a list of the articles in *VF* for 1947–1956; the second contains the titles of books published between 1947 and 1956 and a list (a) of books (b) of articles in the *Voprosy filosofii* and *Filosofskie nauki* for 1957 and 1958. The book titles were listed on the basis of quotations appearing in *VF* and publications of under 100 pages were not included. It is, therefore, a complete bibliography, neither in regard to books nor articles, but it probably includes the most important items. The first issue of *Sovietica* contains a detailed index of subjects and the second a complete index of names for both issues.

For the last twelve years, from 1947 to 1958, *Sovietica* lists rather more than 2,600 titles, including about 500 titles of books (of over 100 pages). This gives an average of about 200 titles a year (including 40 books). But the number of publications is not evenly distributed among the various years and a quantitative progress may be noted. The number of book titles rose from 23 in 1947 to 67 in 1956.

Hence, although the Soviet Union remains rather far behind Western countries as regards the number of philosophic publications, the constant growth of the number of publications indicates that they are not so far behind as one might think and, further, are growing constantly closer. So much for the titles. As regards the size of the editions, the ratio between the Soviet Union and the West is very much in favor of the Soviet Union, since the editions there are often very large. Apart from the 'classics', of which millions of copies are printed, other books as well often appear in very large editions. To quote only a few examples: the second edition of the collective work *On Dialectical Materialism* (1953) (874) amounted to 500,000 copies; the *Short Philosophic Dictionary* (3rd edition) of 1951 (884) appeared in an edition of 500,000 copies; the *Foundations of Marxist Philosophy* (1958) (1961) in an edition of 250,000 copies. Even specialized works are often published in comparatively large editions: for example, 10,000 copies were published of M. E. Omeljanovskij's book on *Lenin and the Physics of the Twentieth Century* in 1947 (876). Even the highly academic collective works, *Problems of Logic* (1955) (1314) and *Problems of Esthetics* (2192) appeared in an edition of 10,000 copies. each In the West philosophical books attain editions of this size only very rarely.

5. Conferences

A special characteristic of philosophic life in the Soviet Union is the great number of conferences at which philosophical problems are discussed. These conferences may be classified as follows.

Firstly, there are from time to time large gatherings of philosophers which are nearly always convened by a high government authority in order to issue important directives. These directives are admittedly dressed up in a wordy discussion entitled "Criticism and Self-Criticism", but the important thing is the line which is promulgated. We mentioned one of these big conferences above (§ 1).

A *second* type of conference is represented by the numerous gatherings which serve the same purpose as those already mentioned, but in which no high officials participate. They are held on the initiative of subordinate organizations and on a purely local basis. The following may serve as examples:

On 13 August 1948 a conference on the situation in biology (644) took place at the Institute of Philosophy, evidently in connection with the Lysenko conference; in the same year a conference took place in Charkov on the subject of physics; in April 1950 at the Institute of Philosophy a conference took place on *Pravda's* criticism of writers (356(1)); in November 1956 one took place at the Academy of Social Sciences on the resolutions of the Central Committee (300). Above all, a great number of meetings were devoted to the works of the 'genius' Stalin in 1950 and 1952. It is hardly worthwhile listing them in detail (see 356(2), 388, 439(1), 449, 492a).*

A *third* type of conference is represented by the smaller gatherings in which normally only the philosophers of a single city or sometimes only a single institution take part, together with guest speakers. These meetings are devoted to the criticism of a particular work or project. In the Soviet Union philosophers are in the habit of discussing every important publication very meticulously and collective works are often scrutinized in great detail before publication. A book is sometimes printed twice: first in draft form (available only to professors, members of the Institutes and the authorities) and secondly, all over again, for the general public after the draft has been thoroughly discussed. A few examples: a discussion took place at the Academy of Sciences from January 15 to 23 1948 on M. M. Rozental' 's *Marxist Dialectical Method* (329); on A. M. Markov's *On the Micro-World* (569) at the Institute of Philosophy on January 23 1948; on March 26 and 30 1948 at the P. I. on Stepanjan's *From Socialism to Communism* (758); in the same year in the Philosophic Faculty of the

* Sad to say, practically *all* of the representatives of the older generation enthusiastically took part in this degrading cult of the tyrant.

University of Moscow on a prospectus of the *History of Philosophy* (582(13)); on March 10 1950 at the P. I. on I. V. Kuznecov's *Principle of Relativity in Contemporary Physics* (432(4)); in October 1950 at the P. I. on the draft of the book on *Basic Laws of Logic* (787(4)) by N. I. Kondakov; in 1951 at the P. I. on the collective work on *Historical Materialism* (552) edited by F. V. Konstantinov; 600 persons are said to have taken part in this conference; on September 26 1951 at the P. I. on the syllabus for ethics (137); at the end of the same year on a prospectus of the book on *Dialectical Materialism and Contemporary Science* (529). At the end of 1954 no less than four such meetings took place to sit in judgment on the second edition of the book on *Historical Materialism* (441, 605, 634, 779) which has already been mentioned; on November 30 and December 18 1956 Y. G. Baskakov's book on *Černyševskij* (1014(2)) was discussed; and so on.

In the *fourth* place, it is customary in the Soviet Union to hold ceremonial conferences in honor of deceased philosophers or revolutionaries. One such conference in the Academy of Sciences (1948) (607) was devoted to the 100th anniversary of the *Communist Manifesto* and in the same year the Institute of Philosophy held a special meeting in honor of Belinski (604). On January 21 1949 the Marx-Engels-Lenin Institute (IMEL) held a special meeting to mark the 25th anniversary of the death of Lenin (67,164). The same Institute and the Academy of Sciences devoted another meeting to the 40th anniversary of *Materialism and Empirio-Criticism* (583,18). In 1949 conferences were held to celebrate the bicentenary of the birth of Radiščev (582,20) and the centenary of the birth of Pavlov (6). The Institute of Language and Thought met – very imprudently – to commemorate the 15th anniversary of the death and the 85th anniversary of the birth of N. Ja. Marr who was to be denounced in June of the same year (660(1)).

Voltaire was commemorated on May 29 1953 (740); the 30th anniversary of the death of Lenin was commemorated on January 18 1954 (Acad. of Sciences). The Academy devoted a similar meeting to Ludwig Feuerbach on October 15 1954 (63(1)) to commemorate the 150th anniversary of his birth. At the end of 1955 there was a commemoration of Gassendi (705). These conferences are by no means merely formal occasions. Lectures on philosophy and the history of philosophy are delivered, followed by discussion. For some time now we have been hearing increasingly of a different sort of conference at which neither a philosopher nor a book is discussed, but a group of problems. Thus the Academy of Sciences devoted a meeting in 1951 to the philosophical problems involved in the transformation of Nature (299(1)). In 1956 the editorial staff of *Voprosy filosofii* devoted a similar meeting to the subject of aesthetics (212). In January 1956 a meeting took place at the Institute of Philosophy to discuss the laws of technical progress. On February 13 at the same Institute aesthetics (1549(1)) were discussed again, and about this time a conference on morality (1810) was held at the University of Moscow. In the spring of 1958 an important conference on contradictions (2181(2)) took place in the P. I. and in October another was held on the philosophical problems of physics.

The conferences mentioned here have only been given as examples. The press has also contained reports on many other such meetings and others have no doubt been held apart from those on which reports have appeared. It should also be noted that apart from oral discussion, written discussions have also often taken place, such as those devoted to Markov in 1948–1949 and to logic in 1950–1951.

The general impression one gets from reading the reports on these conferences may be summed up as follows: 1] It is certain that Soviet philosophers discuss a great deal – probably more than their Western colleagues; 2] The level of discussion has risen considerably in the last twelve years; there is now less invective and more objective argument; 3] The conferences seem to be developing more in the direction of genuine philosophic discussion and away from the communication and elaboration of Party instructions.

One characteristic of Soviet philosophers is their close cooperation with the scientists. Light on the extent of this cooperation is thrown by a report by M. T. Iovčuk and G. A. Kursanov on the philosophical seminars for scientists held in Sverdlovsk in 1951 (273). From this report we learn that one such seminar for physicists held 15 sessions, with an attendance of 150 to 200. The seminar for philosophical problems of chemistry held eight meetings in the academic year 1951–1952, the philosophical seminar of the geologists 11 meetings, with an attendance of 55 to 65. A similar seminar for biologists met once a month and between 40 and 80 took part. Finally, the philosophical seminar for mathematicians is said to have held ten meetings with an attendance of between 50 and 60. This seminar was held under the auspices of the State University whereas the others were organized by the Urals branch of the Academy of Sciences. As is clear from the report, all these seminars had serious ends in view and were attended by numerous leading scientists.

6. The Dogmatic Ties

Soviet philosophy is tied to a dogma. It is a kind of thinking which has its positive foundations and its limits imposed on it from the outside, by an authority alien to philosophy.

In this respect it is possible to discern a certain degree of progress in recent times. Some philosophers only retain the letter of Communist dogma, and latterly some of the 'classics' have even been criticized directly. And although 'revisionism' has been much attacked, some Soviet philosophers are conducting their criticism with methods more rational than mere vituperation.

In spite of all these signs of change, however, there can be no suggestion that free, undogmatic philosophy is as yet feasible in the Soviet Union. The authorities have proclaimed quite openly and bluntly, until quite recently, the absolutely binding force of Communist dogma. Among the philosophers themselves efforts are being made to obtain freedom from this enslavement, but all such attempts, even the most radical, always take the form of an interpretation of rather than an attack on the dogma. A classical example is that of the Soviet logicians who take an anti-dialectical, Aristotelian stand against 'dialectical' nonsense in logic. These philosophers are aiming fundamentally at a complete rejection of some of the basic theses of Dialectical Materialism, but their attacks always take the form of a 'deeper interpretation' of Dialectical Materialism.

Since the fact that Soviet philosophers are enslaved to dogma has often been questioned in recent times, we propose to quote a few official pronouncements on the subject from recent years.

The following resolution was adopted at the Twentieth Congress of the Communist Party of the Soviet Union:

"The Party Congress instructs the Central Committee to guard the purity of Marxist-Leninist theory like the apple of its eye." (March 1956).

This led to the Central Committee ordering the introduction of a course on Dialectical Materialism in all higher schools (see 1767).

In the Declaration of the twelve Communist parties which met in Moscow in November 1957, to celebrate the 40th anniversary of the October Revolution, we read:

"Dialectical Materialism is the theoretical foundation of Marxism-Leninism. This ideology or conception of the world reflects a universal law of development in Nature, society and human thought. This conception applies to the past, present, and future. Dialectical Materialism is opposed by metaphysics and idealism. If a Marxist political party does not base its analyses on dialectics and materialism, the inevitable result will be the rise of one-sidedness and subjectivism and the ossification of all thought." *(Pravda* November 22 1957).

Khrushchov himself has formulated this viewpoint with all the clarity which could be desired. Here are a few of his statements:

"The enemies of Communism ... wanted to use the criticism of the cult of the personality of Stalin against the bases of our system *(stroja)* against the principles of Marxism-Leninism; but, my dear sirs, nothing has or will come of it." (January 17 1957, see N.S. Khrushchov: *Za pročnyj mir i mirnoe sosuščestvovanie.* M., Gospolitizdat, 1958, p. 13).

"We are led by the teaching of Marxism-Leninism." *(loc. cit.)*

"We will firmly and consistently bring to life the great ideas of Marxism-Leninism". (February 18 1957, *op. cit.* p. 16).

"Stalin furthered, with devotion, ... the work of Marxism-Leninism, and we will not abandon Stalin to the enemy." (February 18 1957, *op cit.* p. 21).

"In all its activity ... our Party is led by the doctrine of Marxism-Leninism." (April 15 1957, *op. cit.* p. 27).

"Our parties must turn against and demask the pseudo-Communists so that they do not pervert Marxist-Leninist theory." (May 10 1957, *op. cit.* p. 49.

"I would say that the comparison with a marching company of soldiers is relevant here. When the entire company is marching in step *(v nogu)*, with the exception of one soldier, then that soldier must drop out of the ranks and go to the rear until he has learned how to march. This is the order of the army. Just so is our attitude toward the problems of Marxism-Leninism. We are very strict when it comes to adherence to the basic principles of Marxism-Leninism and we tolerate no distortions *(izvraš-čenie)* when Marxist-Leninist theory is in question. We will always keep Marxist-Leninist theory pure." *(loc. cit.).*

"What is the basis of the unity of the lands of the great socialist brotherhood? ... the unity of Marxist-Leninist ideology." (November 6 1957, *op cit.* p. 226f.).

"Today more than 950 million men are building, under the banner of Marxism-Leninism, a new life in the lands of socialism." (December 6 1957, *op. cit.* p. 242).
One cannot put it any more strongly or more clearly: Marxism-Leninism and its basis, Diamat, is the *Weltanschauung* of the CPSU and is to be kept pure as the "apple of its eye". It is no wonder, then, that no deviations are to be tolerated: like an army, Khrushchov's 950,000,000 men are to march in dogmatic step. It is a fitting comparison, one which aptly expresses the nature of the dogmatic ties – there is the spirit of iron, military discipline.

7. The 'Classics'

The special mark of Soviet philosophy is that it constantly uses the concept of the so-called 'classics'.
The 'classics' who are now quoted exclusively are Marx, Engels and Lenin. Until February 1956 Stalin was also a 'classic'. We know of no single philosophical text in which any other author is so called – in particular, this applies to Mao Tse-tung.
The rôle of the 'classics' may be described as follows. *Firstly,* they are regarded as great, highly gifted, leading revolutionary thinkers. They mark

the beginning of a completely new era in human thought. *Secondly,* they are always being quoted in all conceivable contexts. In this respect, however, there has been some progress – for some years now articles have been appearing in which no statement at all or only very few have been quoted from the 'classics'.

Thirdly, until recently it was forbidden to contradict the classics: what they had said was regarded as absolute truth. In this respect, too, there has been some progress in recent times; we know of two texts in which Soviet philosophers have attacked a classic – Engels – and have declared that he made false statements. The first of these is by E. A. Asratjan (39(2)), and contains a criticism of a statement on the psycho-physical problem; the second is a report on a controversy by A. Kolman (2181(2) p. 165f.), and this deals with an ontological problem. It is a striking fact that although other philosophers defended Engels (thus in the case of Asratjan: A. G. Rudov (598) and A. S. Piette (546)), the controversy was relatively polite. It should be noted, however, that in both cases what was criticized was a single statement and, at any rate in the case of Kolman, the critic emphasized that in the text under discussion Engels had contradicted his own general doctrine.

The present situation may perhaps be described in the following way. The teaching of the classics continues to be regarded as absolutely true but it is the whole doctrine rather than individual statements which is so regarded. A few years ago every word of the 'classics' was 'sacred'.

Fourthly, a great deal of Soviet philosophy consists in the interpretation of the "classics" and in attempts to adapt their teaching to the facts of science. Two examples may be cited to illustrate the above points. First, we propose to give some statements made by Soviet logicians in 1950–1951 about Stalin's excursion into linguistics; then we shall give some statistics on the number of quotations from the 'classics' that appeared in the two years 1950 and 1958.

The cringing attitude of the Soviet logicians in 1950–1951 is profoundly shocking. And, although Stalin's ukase in fact gave them the chance to attack the 'dialectical' nonsense, it is sufficient to read the following passages to realize how un-free their thinking or at any rate their speaking was at that time.

K. S. Bakradze: "Since the new works of Comrade Stalin on linguistics

have appeared, which are intended to provide the basis not only for So-
viet-Marxist linguistics but for all scientific knowledge, many debatable
questions of logic have been automatically settled." (49(1)).

This word "automatically" – from the mouth of Bakradze of all men – is
truly monstrous.

V. I. Čerkesov: "Comrade Stalin has proved with complete clarity that
there is no 'class-bound' language and grammar ... That which Comrade
Stalin said about grammar is also true of logic." (129(1)).
M. S. Strogovič: "Due to the indications of Comrade Stalin, this science
(= formal logic) has come back into its own." (669).
I. I. Osmakov: "The works of Comrade Stalin on linguistics open up wide
perspectives not only for the development of linguistics but for other
sciences as well, especially logic. Many problems of logic have now become
very clear." (522(3)).

P. S. Popov: "Comrade Stalin's work of genius *Marxism and Questions
of Linguistics* also has a direct bearing on logic." (567(2)).

N. I. Kondakov: Stalin's works on the problem of linguistics were an
enormous help to the logicians. They illuminated the most difficult
problems, including the problems of logic, with the light of Stalin's
genius." (787(4)).

A. O. Makovelskij: "The works of genius of Comrade Stalin on questions
of linguistics enriched Soviet science, including logic. They illuminate, in a
new and profound way, a series of basic questions." (431(2)).

V. M. Boguslavskij: (quoted by M. N. Alekseev) "In his analysis of linguistic phenomena Comrade Stalin exemplifies it (i.e. bolshevik party-
mindedness)." (11(1)).

E. K. Vojšvillo: (quoted by Alekseev): "Since the appearance of Stalin's work
Marxism and Questions of Linguistics all logicians are uniformly of the
opinion that the forms and laws of thought, which are investigated by formal logic, are universally human and proper to all who think." (11(1)).

N. V. Vorobjov: (quoted by Alekseev): "Now, after the work of genius of I. V. Stalin on questions of linguistics, it has become clear that the logical apparatus is as important to thought as is grammar to language." (11(1)).

B. M. Kedrov: "J. Stalin's *Marxism and Questions of Linguistics* is of especially great significance for the elaboration of questions of logic.' (322(7)).

Our second piece of evidence consists in a summary of the quotations (only those which appear with footnote references) in three Soviet publications: two issues of *Voprosy filosofii* (1950, 2 and 3); the text, *Foundations of Marxist Philosophy* (end of 1958); *Voprosy filosofii* and *Filosofskie nauki* for 1958.

	VF 1950			Foundations			VF & FN 1958*		
	num-ber	Percentage of		num-ber	Percentage of		num-ber	Percentage of	
		clas-sics	all		clas-sics	all		clas-sics	all
Marx alone	7	1.2	0.5	20	8.0	5.5	84	11.1	8.4
Marx and Engels	46	7.9	3.3	45	17.9	12.4	133	17.5	13.4
Engels alone	68	11.8	4.9	50	19.9	13.8	105	13.8	10.6
Lenin	167	28.9	12.1	134	53.4	37.0	437	57.6	44.0
Stalin	290	50.2	21.1	2	0.8	0.6	0	0.0	0.0
"Classics"	578	100	41.9	251	100	69.3	759	100	76.4
Others	799	138.2	58.1	111	44.2	30.7	235*	31	23.6
Total	1377		100	362		100	994		100

The figures show that Stalin has fallen away from his dominating position (half of the quotations from the 'classics' and more than one-fifth of all the quotations) to a position of insignificance (less than 1 %). The small rôle that Marx plays among these 'Marxists' is equally obvious. Lenin is now predominant – and he alone is quoted more often than all the other

* Only authors who were quoted more than twice.

'classics' put together. His rôle is even greater than it might seem since the authors we put under 'others' are, for the most part, quoted only so that they might be refuted while Lenin is *always* cited to support the proposed thesis. The most impressive fact, however, is that the number of quotations from the 'classics', has not dropped but rather risen; in the first sample they constitute only a little over 2/5th, in the second they form nearly 70% of all the quotations.

Finally, a few figures from *Novye knigi* (1959, 14) on the editions of Lenin's works: "The works of Vladimir Il'ič Lenin were published in the Soviet Union since 1918 7,701 times in 62 languages of the nations of the SU and 26 foreign languages with a total of 301,015,000 copies: in Russian, 2378 times with a total of 227,886,000 copies; in the languages of the other nations of the SU, 4313 times, totaling 56, 510,000 copies; in foreign languages, 1010 times with a total of 16,619,000 copies. ... Four editions of the (collected) works of Vladimir Il'ič have been published in the SU and the Institute of Marxism-Leninism has already published three volumes of the fifth and complete – in 55 volumes – edition. Among the single works of V.I. Lenin, the most frequently published have been: *State and Revolution* (185 times in 46 languages, totalling 6,440,000 copies); ... *Imperialism as the Highest Phase of Capitalism* (198 times in 49 languages with a total of 3,091,000 copies); ... *Materialism and Empiriocriticism* (103 times in 23 languages, totalling 5,034,000 copies)."

8. 'Criticism and Self-Criticism'

The enslavement of the Soviet philosopher consists not merely in the fact that he is bound to recognize the absolute truth of the 'classics' but also that he is forced to submit to the official interpretation of their teaching. That this is so is clear from the specifically Communist institution of 'Criticism and Self-Criticism'. These words have a completely different meaning from that which they bear in the West; they imply submission to the official interpretation of the teaching of the 'classics'. The 'critic' states the 'line' of the Party organs; the self-critic openly states that he has erred and he promises to mend his ways. Needless to say, it often happens that the critics really are in agreement with the Party line; whether this is so in the case of the 'self-critics' is more doubtful. If one remembers that the 'criticism' is often given by quite unqualified, not to say primitive men, against outstanding specialists (for example, in the case of Majstrov against Janovskaja or Maksimov against Markov, etc.) it is difficult to assume that the 'self-criticism' can represent the speaker's inner convictions. It is often a case of subjection to an alien human authority – against the speaker's conscience. The impressive fact, however, is that some of these 'conversions' do appear to be genuine. One such case was probably that of Prof. L. S. Rubinštejn (Jan. 1960), the leading Soviet psychologist, who published an article (2044(2)) after the Pavlovian Conference in 1952, which to all appearances testified to an inner conversion to the Party line.

As in other contexts it is possible to observe a certain degree of progress in recent years. Even in 1948 Prof. V. F. Asmus is said, at a conference specially convened to criticize his work, not only not to have acknowledged his guilt but to have dared to defend himself (522(1)). The subject was "formalism in logic", a thesis which at that time was considered simply a deviation. We find a similar phenomenon among the physicists. It looked as if the same fate was being prepared for them in 1950 as the geneticists underwent in 1948 as a result of the Lysenko Affair. But, the physicists defended themselves and refused to practise self-criticism. Finally, after two leading logicians, K. S. Bakradze and N. I. Kondakov, were sharply criticized by the editors of *VF* in 1955 (2029(4)) (it has to be remembered that *VF* is an official organ), the accused not only defended themselves but were even allowed to publish their replies (49(3), 347).

As far as the immediate past is concerned the impression one gets may be summed up as follows. There are in the Soviet Union a number of philosophers who regard enslavement to the official ideology as inadmissible and are striving to reduce it to a minimum. So much appears to be beyond all doubt. It is more difficult, however, to define the extent to which they have so far succeeded. That there has been a certain amount of progress seems, again, to be certain – but it is highly likely that the results are still very far from what these thinkers themselves would like.

9. The Philosophic Style

Soviet philosophy has its own style which is in many respects quite different from that of Western Europe or of the USA. Some of its characteristics are to be evaluated as entirely positive whilst others are awkward and one might say downright barbaric.

Thus, every unbiased reader of Soviet philosophical literature is struck by its *didactic character*, i. e. the really exemplary clarity of formulation and the skillful use of concrete examples.

Another positive trait of this philosophy is its attitude which we might, pending later restriction of the term, call *scientific*. Up to recent years the knowledge of Soviet philosophers was quite restricted – thus, we found and occasionally still find really monstrous things in reference to doctrines treated, e.g. Alexander is put in the same camp with Cassirer and labeled 'idealist', or alizarine is used to refute Kant, etc. But even in Soviet philosophy's darkest hour, when the general level of education was still quite low, there was an evident *fundamentalist tendency*. Quotations were made wherever possible, from the original source, documentation provided and an evident effort made to give exact bibliographical data. In other words, the majority of Soviet philosophical publications belong not to a 'poetic' but to a, in the above sense, 'scientific' philosophy – to a philosophy rather of scientists than of novelists.

At the same time this philosophy is scarred by numerous negative traits. We have already mentioned the first of these – i.e. its 'theological' character and its 'quotationism'. Nevertheless, we pointed out above that two changes seem to be under way in reference to this characteristic. First, 'quotationism' is more and more set aside because, instead of working on the basis of the single pronouncements of the 'classics', one takes the *sense* of their works as a whole; hence, once in a while we now find criticisms of some of the single statements. Secondly, there are more and more articles in which the argument 'from Scripture' is simply not used. But, these remain exceptions.

Another trait which is negative and unscientific is a rugged, naive and repulsive *nationalism*. At the beginning of the present period there was a real crisis on this question when Soviet philosophers, taking the lead from A. A. Ždanov, (796(2)), condemned one another for 'a cringing attitude' (293) toward foreign philosophy. An entire discussion (if it can be so called – it was more a series of name-calling articles) was occasioned by the article of Z. A. Kamenskij (302(2)) who took a moderate stand on the question of patriotism (40(1), 131, 237, 332, etc.).

The situation today seems to be somewhat better. Nevertheless, this nationalism has by no means disappeared. For example: it is really astonishing that a man like V. F. Asmus designates the works, few and certainly not first-class (though sometimes worthwhile), of Soviet mathematical logicians as 'especially important' and makes of them a 'Soviet school' (in *Questions of Logic*, 1314, p. 193). Similar are the statements of another serious Soviet thinker, L. S. Rubinštejn, who characterized the entirety of non-Soviet psychology as 'idealist'. (2044(2)). It should be noted that behind the opposition 'Marxist' – 'bourgeois' is often hidden the opposition 'Soviet' – 'foreign'.

Perhaps this is the occasion to make a suggestion to Soviet philosophers. They have, in very difficult circumstances, produced some worthwhile results, often risking their lives for pure philosophy. Soviet philosophy has now become an important element in contemporary thought. It is the philosophy of a great people. There is no reason why its exponents should suffer from a feeling of inferiority and try to compensate in a naively nationalistic way. Only small men and small nations have to be nationalist in this way. It would be very welcome if Soviet philosophers would become conscious of this fact and begin to use another style.

A further negative trait of Soviet philosophy was the *name-calling*. In this respect we may note that not all philosophers lowered themselves to this use of barbaric language. And, further, in the course of 1956 to 1959 I did not find one single name-calling *title* in the VF. *

One could conclude from this that Soviet philosophy – and, perhaps, the SU as a whole – has freed itself from this habit. To this must be said that it seems that men who are conscious of the methodological impropriety of name-calling (it is, as a matter of fact, pre-scientific and can only make things worse) are now in control of the publications. Nevertheless, those very men who were the worst in this respect a few years ago are still there and some of them – like Omeljanovskij – are in key-positions. One can hope that the situation will not become worse. But, such a turn is not excluded.

* Even more striking is the following personal experience. B. Korolev and A. Golota devoted an extensive review (in *Kommunist* 1959, 4, pp. 148–154) to the big *Handbuch des Weltkommunismus,* edited by myself and Prof. G. Niemeyer. The review is entitled, "One More Normal Bankruptcy of the Ideologists of Anti-Communism" – but in the text I found not one instance of name-calling. This is all the more astonishing in view of the fact that this 'handbook' is certainly not pleasant for Soviet Communists since it is, to use the expression of the reviewers, "a veritable Bible of anti-Communism", therefore, not a purely philosophic work.

Finally, I would note the *verbosity* of many Soviet philosophers as a negative characteristic. Although we do find a number of scholars who write beautifully, many of them and above all the reactionaries write with a real oriental prolixity so that the reading of their works is boring and a simple waste of time. In addition, there is the tendency in the SU to mix in considerations which have little or nothing to do with philosophy – thus, many articles in *VF* and *Filosofskie nauki* deal with purely political, economic, artistic matters and things of this type.

10. Division

The 'classical' version divides all of philosophy into Dialectical and Historical Materialism. As a matter of fact, the development of Soviet philosophy has rendered this simplest schema obsolete. Already in 1949 a conference of the directors of the *'kafedry'* for Marxism-Leninism (8 to 15 July, (522(2))) put forth the following division as being suitable:

1. Diahistomat   5. Psychology
2. History of Foreign Philosophy   6. Philosophy of Science
3. History of Philosophy in the SU   7. Aesthetics
4. Logic   8. Pedagogy

This scheme is more or less exactly followed at least in the division of bibliographies. The following table gives the percentage distribution of the single disciplines in two such bibliographical lists (for 1956 and 1958 in 2029(7) and 3845(3)):

	%
Diamat	5.9
Logic	4.7
Phil. of Science	3.5
Histomat	16.5
Ethics	5.9
Aesthetics	20.0
Scientific Atheism	16.5
History of Phil.	27.0
	100.0

11. The Main Tendencies

A new phenomenon in Soviet philosophy is the strong emergence of various tendencies often sharply opposed to one another; it is possible to speak of real philosophical schools. There are in the main three such tendencies: we shall call them the reactionary, Hegelian and Aristotelian tendencies.

1] *The Reactionaries:* First of all there is a prominent and numerous group of men belonging almost entirely to the older generation who now occupy the key positions in philosophical life and who adhere to the reactionary line in philosophy. A typical and blatant example is A. A. Maksimov, who is always denouncing his colleagues. Another is M. M. Rozental', a leading philosopher with a mania for quoting the 'classics', co-author of the *Short Philosophic Dictionary* and also denouncer of other philosophers. These are only two among many others who could be mentioned.

We have called this tendency reactionary because its representatives try stubbornly to hinder all progress and to preserve the old theories of Dialectical Materialism. In every discussion the representatives of this school speak against everything that is in any respect new in philosophy; against the recognition of the theory of relativity; against formal logic; against the new interpretation of contradictions, etc. Very important because of its prominent position, it is philosophically not very significant. The men who form this group do not appear to think much and it is impossible to learn much from them.

2] *The Hegelians:* In our view a distinction should be made between the reactionaries and those philosophers who, though opposed to the onrush of new, scientific, Aristotelian ideas, use argument rather than quotation to support their position and argue from a well-conceived dialectical (i.e. basically Hegelian) point of view. The mathematician-philosopher, A. D. Aleksandrov, may be cited as a typical example. His comments on formal logic (7) are unacceptable from a scientifically logical standpoint but only because they are Hegelian. As such they are no worse than similar theories which one often comes across in the West. There are few quotations in Aleksandrov and his attitude in the discussion on the theory of relativity was certainly rational and courageous. Another example is A. A. Karapetjan, the author of a fine work on Kant (1771) written from

the Hegelian angle. A third example of genuinely Hegelian thought is to
be found in the writings of A. N. Uemov (2160(1)).

3] *The Aristotelians:* There is also – and perhaps above all – an Aristotelian
tendency in Soviet philosophy. This is not surprising, since the so-called
'materialism' is basically an interpretation of Aristotelianism: Aristotle
was also highly esteemed by Lenin. Obviously, Aristotelianism fits in
with the new kind of technical thinking much better than the reactionary
nonsense and also better than Hegelianism. K. S. Bakradze is probably
the leading Aristotelian. With great patience and much courage he has
always clearly expounded the Aristotelian interpretation of logic, even
going so far as to reject 'dialectical' logic, which he acknowledges only
as a purely epistemological theory and nothing more. Another Aristotelian is the Nestor of Soviet logicians, Prof. V. F. Asmus. His criticism of
the contemporary 'idealist' philosophies of logic is thoroughly Aristotelian; and so is his courageous and triumphant defence of formal logic.
B. M. Kedrov, probably the most important contemporary Soviet
thinker, is not far from this point of view. The only other thinker we propose to mention is I. V. Blauberg, who is notable for his reinterpretation
of the law of universal relationships. Last but not least there are the
mathematical logicians who – like A. A. Zinoviev – had the courage to
deny that there are any genuine contradictions in existence. One's general
impression is that this group is not only the largest of the three but also
has the largest number of younger thinkers.

This classification of Soviet philosophy must be regarded as a provisional
one – more a working hypothesis than a rigid fact. Up to now it has been
possible for individual Soviet thinkers to express their views clearly only
within a limited field. It often happens that a thinker who on one topic
has advocated the Aristotelian approach makes extremely un-Aristotelian
statements on another subject. The difference between the reactionaries
and the two other groups seems to be more acute than that which divides
the latter groups from one another. There is, for example, no possible
bridge between the nonsense on contradictions (1961, p.256f.) perpe-
trated in the *Osnovy* of 1958 and the deeply conceived scientific attitude
of an A. Kolman and an A. A. Zinoviev (2181(2)); similarly, the loquaci-
ous B. M. Moročnik (482(2)) and the thoughtful Hegelian A. D. Aleksandrov (7(2)) belong to two quite different worlds. What B. M. Kedrov
once wrote (322(3)) about A. A. Maksimov (for which he was made to

suffer), demonstrates this unbridgeable gulf between the adherents of
barbaric reactionary nonsense and the philosophers. Here too, however,
one has to be careful. We know of at least one case, that of G. A. Kursanov,
in which we have been able to discern a clear transition from reactionary
stupidity to respectable philosophical work. As we have said, the difference between the thinkers I have called Hegelians and Aristotelians
are less clearly marked and less consistent. Both groups are adherents of
Dialectical Materialism, which is an irrational amalgamation of the two
philosophies. Whilst some of these thinkers have succeeded in attaining
complete clarity on some questions, they often fail and the picture they
produce remains in some respects obscure.

III. DIALECTICAL MATERIALISM ACCORDING TO THE 'OSNOVY' (1958)

In this section we offer a summary of the most important theses of the
newest official textbook of Soviet dogma, namely the *"Osnovy marksistskoj filosofii"* which was published by the Academy of Sciences of the SU
under the editorship of F. V. Konstantinov in 750,000 copies. *
The basic problem of philosophy is the question on the relationship
between thought and being, between spirit and nature, on which of the
two is primary (p.10). There are two principal answers to this question:
the materialists give the priority to matter; they are of the opinion that
no one made the world, that nature is eternal. The idealists attribute
priority to thought or 'spirit'. A compromise position, i.e. dualism, is
contradictory (p.11). Materialism is vulgar (or mechanist) or Marxist
(p.19). The weakness of vulgar materialism lies in the use of the metaphysical method – i.e. that it treats of things without considering their organic
interconnections – which is the contradictory of the dialectical method
(p.20).
The object of philosophy is the investigation of the interconnections and
relationships which are more universal than those which are investigated
by the special sciences (p.24). It investigates the universal laws of all
becoming and of every development (p.25). A non-philosophic special

* For a full resumé of this text with an extensive index, see Bocheński (1959, 2).

science is (against positivism) impossible (p.28). When the scientist passes from the description of facts to the postulation of laws and to theoretical considerations he cannot get along without philosophy, *Weltanschauung*, without a theory of knowledge (p.29).

For the Communist Party questions of *Weltanschauung* are not the private affairs of its members (p.35). The Party considers the defence of the philosophic bases of Marxism a Party affair – it is an ideological monolith (p.35). Marxist philosophy is a Party philosophy. Since, however, the proletariat is interested in knowing the true laws because these are necessary for the transformation of society, the party-mindedness of Marxist philosophy does not contradict its objectivity (p.35/6).

Matter is a philosophic category for the designation of the objective reality which is given to man in sensation and which is copied, photographed, represented in his sensations and which exists independent of him (p.116/7). The sole 'quality' of matter which philosophic materialism is held to recognize is the quality of being objective reality, of existing outside of our knowledge (p.119). In opposition to metaphysical materialism, Diamat rejects the conception of 'necessary and immutable essences of things' and of a 'completely simple substance'. Matter is uncreatable in profundity (p.121). Matter is eternal, endless, infinite. But, every thing is changeable, limited, contingent (p.127). Matter is not homogeneous and determined by a single quality *(odnokačestvennoe)* (p.127).

As science has shown, all in nature is in motion (p.127/8). Motion is not accidental – it is an eternal existential form of matter (p.128). Diamat understands as 'motion' not just the mechanical movement of bodies in space, but every change in general (p.128). The following basic forms of motion can be distinguished: 1] the motion of bodies in relation to other bodies in space; 2] the forms of motion which are investigated by physics, e.g. thermal and electromagnetic phenomena such as light, etc.; 3] chemical processes; 4] biological forms of motion; 5] social events, the history of human society (p.128/9). Every form of motion is inseparably bound up with a certain form of matter (p.129). There can be no matter without motion and no motion without matter (p.132).

Space is an objective and real existential form of self-moving matter (p.138). Time is an objective, real, existential form of self-moving matter (p.139). In the world there is nothing but self-moving matter and self-moving matter cannot move itself other than in space and time (p.139).

The unity of the world does not consist in its being – for it must be before being so – but in its materiality. There is nothing in the world, and there will never be anything in the world, which is not self-moving matter or a simple product of self-moving matter. Therein lies the unity of the world (p.158).

Consciousness is a higher product of matter, of nature. The opinion which holds it to be a quality of an immaterial substance, the 'soul', is fantastic and has been refuted by science (p.159). Consciousness is no special form of matter which has been created by the brain, as the vulgar materialists would have it. Consciousness has no physical qualities as bodies have (p.160). Consciousness is a product of the brain – a function of the brain; the brain is the organ of consciousness, of thought (p.162). Physiological processes and thought are not two parallel processes, but a single process whose inner content is consciousness. Therefore, consciousness is inseparable from matter (p.163).

The senses are the elementary forms of consciousness, upon which all the others are built (p.167). Since man is not only a biological but also a social being (p.171), his brain can form representations or pictures of objects which are not present to the senses (p.172), and can form abstract concepts (p.173) and scientific theories (p.173). These are all reflections of the real world. All matter has the property of reflecting others (p.175). The specific form of this reflection is, in living organisms, the reflex, the reaction to a signal-system (p.178). Human reflection is differentiated by the fact that the second signal-system plays a part; this involves the signal of the signal, i.e. language (p.179).

Sensations are pictures or copies of, and not conventional symbols or hieroglyphs for, material things (p.183). Sensation is a subjective, ideal picture of the objective world. It has a content which is independent of the consciousness of man. This content which reflects the external world is called 'objective truth' (p.186).

Universal, abstract thinking in concepts, which is expressed with the help of words, is proper only to man (p.188). Thought and language are social products, They could not have grown up in isolation. They are important tools for material production (p.189). Language is the immediate reality of consciousness. Reality and consciousness are inseparable (p.190).

The world is a totality in which the separate parts, processes and phenomena are inter-connected (p.194). All which happens in the world, all changes, come about as a result of the activity of causes. There are no uncaused phenomena; though, we do not know all causes (p. 195). Philosophers who recognize the objectivity of this proposition – the law of causality – are determinists; those who deny it are indeterminists. Determinism leaves no place for God, miracles, etc. (p.196). The relationship between cause and effect has the character of inter-action (p.201).

Law is that inter-connection of phenomena, which is essential. By 'essence' is understood the inner, by 'chance' the outer – this not in the spatial sense but in reference to the meaning for the character of the object (p.203). Diamat teaches that the individual as well as the universal is objective – both exist only in inseparable unity with one another (p.205). Nature sets itself no goals. Darwin correctly explained the teleology of the organism through causality (p.212). Diamat excludes neither goals nor the free activity of man. Fatalism is as foreign to Diamat as is subjectivism. For, if human goals are based on the knowledge of the laws of the development of the world, the realization of these goals leads to the domination of the laws of nature and society (p.212/3).

Necessity is what results from the essence of the thing, from the internal relationships of things. Necessity's cause is in itself, that of chance is in another (p.214). Chance is not un-caused-ness. All that happens by chance has its cause (p.218). In the process of development chance is transformed into necessity and vice versa (p.218).

Reality is realized possibility (p.221). Probability is quantitative characterization of possibility. It expresses not the degree of subjective belief of man, but is a characteristic of the objectively existing relationship between the event and its conditions (p.222). In practice, one should consider real possibility and not that which is formal and abstract. Real possibility is a function of existing conditions (p.223).

The world is matter in motion (p.227). There are two treatments of motion: the first – the metaphysical – considers quantitative changes and rejects the qualitative; the other – the dialectical and sole scientific – treats development as the coming to be of something really new, by force of internal contradictions (p.228/9). The basic laws of the dialectic are: the law of the transition from quantitative changes to qualitative; the law of the unity and fight of contradictions; the law of the negation of negation (p.229). There are other categories of the dialectic such as, content and form, chance and necessity, essence and appearance, etc. (p.230).

Quality is a determination of an object, which is internal to it. Therefore, a qualitative change entails the change of the object in question. One is fully justified in calling quality one of the most essential properties (p.235). Quantity is also a determination of the object, which marks it in respect to the degree of development of its properties (p.236). Quantity can – up to a certain point – be increased or diminished without the object losing its qualitative content (p.237). The law of the transition from quantitative changes to qualitative is a law according to which small and at first insignificant modifications of quantity, when they reach a certain level entail basic, qualitative changes in the object. As a result, objects change when one quality disappears and a new one comes to be (p.241).

Quantitative changes constitute the evolutive type of development and qualitative the revolutionary type (p.243). Revolutionary change is a leap, a break in the continuity of quantitative changes, a transition from one quality to another. Every qualitative change has the character of a leap (p.244). Life and the development of nature are made up of slow evolution plus quick leaps (p.246). Therefore, both vulgar evolutionism, according to which there is only evolution without leaps, and catastrophism, according to which there are only leaps and no evolution, are equally false (p.245). Leaps do not happen always and everywhere in an instant. There are long-lasting leaps (p.247).

Political revolutions completely disappear in socialist society, contrary to antagonistic formations where the leaps have this form (p.253).

There are contradictions in things – not only external, i.e. between different objects, but also internal, i.e. oppositions between contradictory aspects and tendencies in the essence of one and the same object (p.259). A moving body is, in the same instant, in one place in space and not in it, i.e. is elsewhere (p.260). The dialectic (of contradictions) is the 'algebra' of the revolution (p. 261). Development is the conflict of opposites. Without inner contradictions there would be no movement (p. 262). Contradictions are solved in the conflict (p. 264). The law of the unity and conflict of opposites is a law according to which all things, phenomena and processes have internally contradictory aspects and tendencies which are in a battle-situation. This fight provides development with its inner impulse and leads to the aggravation of the oppositions until, finally, they are solved in the degeneration of the old and the coming to be of the new (p.265).

Movement and development are self-movement and self-development (p.267). Matter contains within itself the cause of its development (p.268). Movement is due to the fight of internal contradictions (p.268).

For each type of movement there is a specific type of contradiction (p.273). For example, the expression 'battle' has another meaning in nature and in society (p.274). In the development of society there are two types of contradiction – antagonistic and non-antagonistic (p.275). Antagonistic contradictions are the oppositions of incompatible social forces – they lead to conflict (p.275). Non-antagonistic contradictions are the oppositions of such forces and tendencies as have a common, basic interest alongside of the opposition (p.277).

Content is the base, the principal aspect of the object, which qualitatively determines it and appears in all elements (p.281). Form is the mode of existence of the content, its organisation, its structure, that makes its existence possible (p.281). The contradiction between an old form and a new content leads to conflict between them. This conflict lasts until the old form is replaced by a new one which corresponds to the changed content (p.283).

The law of negation of negation is the law according to which there is a relationship between the negated and the negating such that the dialectical negation is not a simple rejection of all previous development but is that basis of development which accepts and retains all that was positive in the previous stages repeats it on a higher level and, thus, in general has a progressive character (p. 301).

The subjective dialectic (the development of our thinking) is a reflection of the objective dialectic (the development of phenomena of the material world). Correctly conceived, the laws of thought are necessarily in complete correspondence to the laws of nature (p.304). The dialectic includes epistemology and logic (p.304). Correctly understood, the law of contradiction is completely compatible with the recognition of contradictions in the objective world because it, like all logical laws, presents only the simpler relationships between things and represents a certain side or aspect, thereby entailing a fixation (p.307). Formal logic is not the sole science of thought; there is also a dialectical logic whose principle object is the problem of truth and which investigates not the external relations but the laws of the development of all material, natural and spiritual things (p.308). Dialectical logic has no laws other than those of the objective dialectic.

Before sense-experience man has not and cannot have any knowledge of the external world. In this respect empiricism is correct. The subject, reason, thinking is active in knowing. In this reference rationalism is correct (p.311). Empiricism and rationalism are two, one-sided, metaphysical versions of knowledge (p.312). Practice is the basis of human knowledge and the criterion of its truth (p.313). The essence is the inner and relatively constant aspect of objective reality, which determines the nature of the phenomenon in question. On the other hand, appearance is the outer, more mobile and changeable aspect of objective reality. Appearance is the concrete self-indication *(obnaruženie)* of the essence (p.314). The essence is reached by thought while appearances are reached by the senses. The unity of essence and appearance is the objective basis of the unity of the sensible and rational in knowledge (p.316).

Knowledge is a reflection, by man, of nature. But, it is not a simple, direct and total *(celnoe)* reflection – it is a process. There are three elements: 1] Nature, 2] human knowledge, i.e. man's brain, 3] the form of the reflection of nature in human knowledge (p.326). Knowledge progresses from the singular through the particular to the universal (p.327).

Theory is not independent and autonomous. It is a scientific universalization of practice and arises from the needs of the practical activity of man (p.334). Pragmatism, which rejects objective truth, is false.

Truth is a process. The coincidence of thought with the object is a process (p.339). Absolute truth is objective truth in its fullness. This is knowledge which cannot be refuted by the further course of science and practice (p.340). Absolute truth is not simply the object toward which our knowledge strives; in every domain of scientific knowledge there are absolutely true statements (p.340). Relative truth is a knowledge which gives an essentially true reflection of reality; but, the reflection is not complete – it concerns the limits of the known, under certain conditions, in certain contexts (p.340).

READINGS

Guide to Readings: Lehmbruch.
Bibliographies: Soviet: Blakeley, Goerdt; Survey of the literature: Bocheński 1959, 2: Western: Wetter (1956, 1958), Bocheński-Niemeyer, Blakeley (1960), Ballestrem, De George, Müller-Markus (1962).
Basic Work: Wetter 1958 (also 1956).
Principal Soviet Sources: outside of the 'classics' (above all Engels and Lenin), *Voprosy filosofii* (1947 ff.), *Filosofskie nauki* (1958ff.), and *Osnovy*. Other works can be found by consulting VF. Soviet sources are useless in translation because the selection of texts is too often made from a *certain* point of view. The scientific study of Soviet Diamat is not possible without a knowledge of Russian.
Research-Papers and Monographic Presentations have been published by a small group of specialists which includes, among others, Blakeley, Dahm, Fetscher, Lobkowicz, Müller-Markus and Wetter. Source materials can be found in *Europa-Archiv, Ost-Probleme, Soviet Studies, Survey*, etc. There is a specialized journal for Soviet philosophic studies, *Studies in Soviet Thought*. The only series devoted to the thought of the SU and the satellites is 'Sovietica', published by the Institute of East-European Studies in Fribourg (Switzerland).

For specific fields:
Ontology: Dahm (1956, 2; 1957, 1).
Logic: Bocheński-Küng; Dahm (1957, 2); Kline (1949 ff.); Lobkowicz.
Psychology: Bauer; Simon.
Philosophy of Science: Dahm (1956, 1); Müller-Markus (especially 1960); Wetter (above all 1958, 1).

On the other hand the literature in opposition to Diamat is immense. Among the older, there is Berdyaev and Russell; more recently, Acton, Ogierman, de Vries.*)

---

* *Marcuse* occupies a special place since his criticism is purely immanent.

BIBLIOGRAPHY

This bibliography contains only those works used in the text or reading list plus a few which were of special aid to the author. It is in no way a full bibliography on the subject.

ACHMINOV, H.: *Theoretical Problems of Communism and the Twenty-First Party Congress.* In: Bulletin. Inst. for the Study of the USSR 1959.

ACTON, H. B.: *The Illusion of the Epoch. Marxism-Leninism as a Philosophical Creed.* 1955.

AHLBERG, R.:*"Dialektische Philosophie" und Gesellschaft in der Sowjetunion.* 1960.

ALEKSANDROV, G. F. (ed.): *Dialektičeskij materializm.* 1954.

ANDREAS, T.: *Zur Widerlegung des dialektischen und historischen Materialismus.* Ilm. 1954.

BALLESTREM, K. G.: *Bibliography of Recent Western Works on Soviet Philosophy.* In: Studies in Soviet Thought II (1962), 168–173.

BAUER, R. A.: *The New Man in Soviet Psychology.* 1952.

BERDYAEV, N.: *Problèmes du communisme.* 1933.

– *Wahrheit und Lüge des Kommunismus.* 1934.

– *The End of Our Time. With an essay on the Soviet philosophy.* 1935.

– *Les sources et le sens du communisme russe.* 1938.

– *Wandlungen des Marxismus in Rußland.* Schweizer Rundschau. 1948.

BERESTNEV, V. F., P. S. TROFIMOV: *Proekt programmy kursa 'Osnovy marksistsko-leninskoj estetiki'.* VF 1948, 1.

BLAKELEY, TH.: *Philosophical Dissertations in the USSR (1947–1954).* (Ms. in OEI Fribourg, Switzerland).

– *Soviet Scholasticism.* (Sovietica). Dordrecht. 1961.

– *Bibliography of English-language Publications on Communism.* In: Columbia Review (Fribourg). 1960.

– *Is Epistemology Possible in Diamat?* In: Studies in Soviet Thought II (1962), 95–103.

BLAKELEY et al.: *Bibliographie der sowjetischen Philosophie.* 1. *'Voprosy filosofii' 1947–1956* 1959. 2. *Books 1947–1956. Books and Articles 1957–1958* 1959. 3. *Books and Articles 1959–1960.* 1962. 4. *Supplement for the Period 1947–1960.* 1963. 5. *Indices,* to appear (1964). (Sovietica. Veröffentlichungen des Ost-Europa Instituts, Univ. Fribourg, Schweiz).

BOCHENSKI, J. M.: *Die kommunistische Ideologie und die Würde, Freiheit und Gleichheit der Menschen im Sinne des Grundgesetzes . . .* 1956.

- *Die dogmatischen Grundlagen der sowjetischen Philosophie.* (Sovietica. Veröffentlichungen 3). 1959.
- *Einführung in die sowjetische Philosophie der Gegenwart.* In: Aus Politik und Zeitgeschichte. 1959.
- *Philosophy Studies. Subject, Object, and Organisation.* In: Soviet Survey, Jan.–March 1960, 64–74.
- *The Three Components of Communist Ideology.* In: Studies in Soviet Thought II (1962), 7–11.
- *Why Studies in Soviet Philosophy?* In Studies: in Soviet Thought III (1963), 1–10.

BOCHENSKI, J. M., BLAKELEY, T. J.: *Studies in Soviet Thought I.* (Sovietica) Dordrecht. 1961.

BOCHENSKI, J., G. KÜNG: *Bibliographie der sowjetischen mathematischen Logik.* (Ms. in OEI Fribourg, Switz.).

BOCHENSKI, J., G. NIEMEYER (eds.): *Handbuch des Weltkommunismus.* Freiburg-München. 1958.

Bolšaja Sovetskaja Enciklopedia. Ed. 1:1926ff. 2:1950ff.

BUCHHOLZ, A.: *Ideologie und Forschung in der sowjetischen Naturwissenschaft.* Stuttgart. 1953.
- *Über das Entwicklungstempo der Sowjetwissenschaft.* In: Osteuropa-Naturwissenschaft 1959, 2, 93–104.
- *Der Kampf um die bessere Welt. Ansätze zum Durchdenken der geistigen Ost-West-Probleme.* Stuttgart. 1961.

BUKHARIN, N.: *Teorija istoričeskogo materializma.* 1921. Engl. *Historical Materialism.* s.d. French: *Théorie du matérialisme historique.* 1927.

CALVEZ, J.–Y.: *La pensée de Karl Marx.* 1956.

CHAMBRE, H.: *De Karl Marx à Mao Tsé-Tung.* 1959.

COMEY, D. D.: *Two Recent Soviet Conferences on Logic.* In: Studies in Soviet Thought II (1962), 21–36.
- *A Positivist Among the Dialecticians.* In: Studies in Soviet Thought II (1962), 204–219.
- *The Communist Ideology.* Washington. 1959.

CZAPSKI, J.: *Terre inhumaine.* 1949.

DAHM, H.: *Innere Widersprüche der Diamat-Soziologie.* Ost-Probleme 1956.
- *Der Streit um die Materie des Diamat.* Ost-Probleme 1956.
- *Ist die sowjetrussische Dialektik latenter Existentialismus?* Ost-Probleme 1956.
- *Ontologische Aspekte der sowjetischen Dialektik.* Osteuropa 1957.
- *Renaissance der formalen Logik.* Ost-Probleme 1957.
- *Die Sowjetphilosophie in der katholischen Kritik und in Selbstdarstellungen.* In: Die Welt der Bücher 1958.

DALLIN, D. J. and B. I. NIKOLAEVSKI: *Zwangsarbeit in Sowjetrußland.* 1947.

DANZAS, J.: *Sous le drapeau du marxisme.* La Vie Intellectuelle. 1936.

DE GEORGE, R. T.: *Bibliography of Soviet Ethics.* In: Studies in Soviet Thought III (1963), 83–103.

DELBOS, Y.: *L'expérience rouge.* 1933.

DELIMARS, E.: *Le retour de Lyssenko.* In: Le Contrat Social 1960, 2, 83–88.

Dialektičeskij materializm. (ed. Mitin and Ral'cevič). BSE vol. 22.

Diskussija o prirode fizičeskogo znanija. VF 1948, 3.

Diskussija po knige G. F. Aleksandrova 'Istorija zapadnoevropejskoj filosofii' 15–25 ijunja 1947 g. VF 1947, 1.

DOBZANSKIJ, TH.: *N. I. Vavilov, a martyr of Genetics.* The Journal of Heredity. 1947.

DOSEV, P. (PAVLOV, T.): *Teorija otraženija.* 1936.

EDGERTON, W.: *A Soviet History of Philosophy.* 1950.

EHLEN, P.: *Der Atheismus im dialektischen Materialismus.* München. 1961.

ENGELS, FR.: *Dialektika prirody.* (ed. A. A. Maksimov, etc.) 1946.

– *Dialektik der Natur.* (ed. D. Rjasanov.) MEGA 1927.

– *Herrn Eugen Dührings Umwälzung der Wissenschaften.* MEGA (Special issue) 1935; also Zürich 1934 and 1945. (1945 edition quoted here)

– *Ludwig Feuerbach und der Ausgang der klassischen deutschen Philosophie.* 1927.

– s. K. Marx, – Fr. Engels,

FALK, H.: *Die Weltanschauung des Bolschewismus.* Würzburg. 1951.

FETSCHER, I.: *Stalin über dialektischen und historischen Materialismus.* 1956.

– *Die Freiheit im Lichte des Marxismus-Leninismus.* 1959.

– *Von Marx zur Sowjetideologie.* Frankfurt a.M. 1959.

FEUER, L. S.: *Dialectical Materialism and Soviet Science.* In: Philos. of Science 1949.

FEUERBACH, L.: *Sämtliche Werke.* (ed. W. Bolin and F. Jodl). 10 vols. 1903–1911.

FLEISCHER, H.: *The Materiality of Matter.* In: Studies in Soviet Thought II (1962), 12–20.

– *The Limits of 'Party-mindedness'.* In: Studies in Soviet Thought II (1962), 119–131.

– *Die Idee der historischen Notwendigkeit im historischen Materialismus.* In: Studies in Soviet Thought II (1962), 181–203.

– *Auf dem Bauplatz der materialistischen Dialektik.* In: Studies in Soviet Thought II (1962), 269–288.

– *Kleines Textbuch der kommunistischen Ideologie.* (Sovietica) Dordrecht. 1963.

FYFE, J. L.: *The Soviet Genetics Controversy.* Modern Quarterly 1947.

GAGARIN, A. P.: *Pragmatizm na službe imperializma v SŠA.* FZ 1948.

GALLIN, K. G.: *Vysšee obrazovanie i podgotovka kadrov v SSSR*. M. 1958.

GERMAN, L. I.: *Filosofija voinstvujuščego katolicizma*. VF 1948, 3.

Geschichte der Kommunistischen Partei der Sowjetunion (Bolshevik) – Kurzer Lehrgang. Berlin, SWA-Verlag 1947 (German transl. of *'Istorija partii*...).

GITERMANN, V.: *Ist Sowjetunion eine Rechtsstaat?* Rote Revue 1938.

GLEZERMAN, G. E.: *Bazis i nadstrojka v sovetskom obščestve*. 1954.

GLUŠČENKO, I. JA.: *Protiv idealizma i metafiziki v nauke o nasledstvennosti*. VF 1948, 4.

GOERDT, W.: *Fragen der Philosophie. Ein Materialbeitrag zur Erforschung der Sowjetphilosophie im Spiegel der Zeitschrift "Voprosy filosofii" 1947–1956*. Köln. 1960.

GORSKIJ, D. P.: *Logika*. ed. 2. 1955.

GREGOIRE, F.: *La pensée communiste*. 3 vols. Louvain. 1953.

GURIAN, W.: *Der Bolschewismus*. 2. A. 1932. (French 1938).

HARPER, J.: *Lenin als Philosoph*. (Bibl. der Räterkorrespondenz 1). 1936. (s. E. J. Walter in Rote Revue 1939, 223).

HAZARD, J. N.: *Soviet Legal Philosophy*. 1957.

HOMMES, J.: *Der technische Eros. Das Wesen der materialistischen Geschichtsauffassung*. Freiburg. 1955.

HOOK, S.: *On the Battlefield of Philosophy*. In: Partisan Review 1949 (March).
– *Reason, Social Myths and Democracy*. New York. 1950.

HUNT, R. N. C.: *The Theory and Practice of Communism*. London. 1951.
– *Marxism Past and Present*. New York. 1954.
– *Books on Communism*. London. 1959.

Istorija vsesojuznoj kommunističeskoj partii (bolševikov). Kratkij kurs... Odobren CK VKP(b) 1938 god. Ogiz-Gospolitizdat 1943.

JOAD, C. E. M.: *Guide to the Philosophy of Morals and Politics*. 1940.

JORAVSKY, D.: *Soviet Marxism and Natural Science(1917–1932)*. London.1961.

JORDAN, Z. A.: *Philosophy and Ideology. The Development of Philosophy and Marxism-Leninism in Poland since the Second World War*. (Sovietica) Dordrecht. 1963.

KALININ, M.: *O kommunističeskom vospitanii*. (ed. 3) 1947.

KAMMARI, M. D.: *Princip bolševistskoj partijnosti v ocenke istoričeskix dejatelej*. VF 1947, 2.

KANAPA, J.: *Bilan des éditions marxistes*. In: Europe 1947 (14).

KLINE, G. L.: *Spinoza in Soviet Philosophy*. 1952.
– (Review of the first edition of this book) Journal of Philos. 1952.
– (Reviews of works on logic) Journ. of Symb. Logic 1952, 1953.
– *A Philosophical Critique of Soviet Marxism*. In: The Review of Metaphysics, Sept. 1955, 90–105.

– *Recent Soviet Philosophy.* Ann. Amer. Acad. Polit. & Soc. Science. 1956.
– (Review of Wetter, *Dialectical Materialism* 1958) Soviet Studies 1959.
– *Fundamentals of Marxist Philosophy.* In: Soviet Survey, Oct.–Dec. 1959, 58–62.
– *Spinoza East and West. Six Recent Studies in Spinozist Philosophy.* In: The Journal of Philosophy 1961, 13, 346–355.
KLUŠČECKIJ, A. V.: *Die marxistisch-sowjetische Konzeption des Menschen im Lichte der westlichen Philosophie.* 1956.
K. V.: *Protiv nizklopoklonstva pered buržuaznoj filosofiej.* VF 4, 1948.
LANGDON-DAVIES, J.: *Russia Puts the Clock Back. A study of Soviet science and some British scientists.* 1949.
LANGE, G.: *Marxismus Leninismus Stalinismus. Zur Kritik des dialektischen Materialismus.* Stuttgart. 1955.
LASERSON, M. M.: *La sociologie russe.* In: *La sociologie au XXe siècle.* (ed. G. Gurvitch and W. E. Moore) 1947.
LENIN: *Sočinenija.* (ed. V. V. Adorackij etc.) ed. 4. 35 vols. 1941–1951.
– *Ausgewählte Werke.* Moskau 1946. (2 vols).
– *Materialismus und Empiriokritizismus. (Soč.* vol. 13) 1927 and 1945.
– *Filosofskie tetrady.* (ed. Adorackij and W. G. Sorin) 1933.
– *Marx-Engels-Marxisme* (selections) Moscow 1947 (contains several works not included in '*Ausgewählte Werke*' (1946)). Among which (often quoted):
– *Du rôle du matérialisme militant* (1922).
LEHMBRUCH, G.: *Kleiner Wegweiser zum Studium der Sowjetideologie.* 1958.
LEONOV, M. A.: *O nekotoryx voprosax dialektiki v rannyx rabotax tovarišča Stalina.* Izv. Ak. Nauk SSSR, Ser. ist. i filos. 1947.
– *Marksistskij dialektičeskij metod.* 1947.
– *Očerk dialektičeskogo materializma.* 1948.
LOBKOWICZ, N.: *Das Widerspruchsprinzip in der neueren sowjetischen Philosophie.* (Sovietica). 1960.
– *Marxismus-Leninismus in der ČSR.* (Sovietica) Dordrecht. 1962.
– *Philosophy in Czechoslovakia Since 1960.* In: Studies in Soviet Thought III (1963), 11–32.
LONDON, I. D.: *Russian Psychology and Psychiatry.* In: Soviet Science 1952.
LORIMER, FR.: *The Population of the Soviet Union.* Geneva. 1946.
MARCUSE, H.: *Soviet Marxism. A critical analysis.* 1958.
MARKOV, M. A.: *O prirode fizičeskogo znanija.* VF 1947, 2.
MARX, K.–FR. ENGELS: *Historisch-kritische Gesamt-Ausgabe.* (publ. by Marx-Engels-Lenin-Institut, Moscow and Frankfurt a/M) 1927ff. Including: – *Das kommunistische Manifest.* MEGA I, 6, 1932. Many other editions, e.g. Zürich 1945.

– *Das Kapital. Kritik der politischen Okonomie.* (vol. 1:1867, ed. 2, 1872: vol. 2:1885, vol. 3:1894 – edited by Engels). Many new editions especially of vol. 1, e.g. Berlin 1932.

MAO TSE-TUNG: *On contradiction.* Peking. 1952.

MASLINA, M. N.: *Za bolševistskuju partijnost' v voprosax psixologii.* VF 1948, 4.

MEYER, A. G.: *Marxism. The unity of theory and practice.* 1954.

– *Leninism.* Cambridge, Mass. 1957.

MICHE, G.: *Manuale di filosofia bolscevica.* 1945.

MIČURINEC; *Protiv propagandy idealizma.* VF 1948, 4.

MILLER, J. and M.: *Andrei Ždanov's Speech to the Philosophers.* Soviet Studies 1949, I.

MITIN, M. B. *Dialektičeskij i istoričeskij materializm.* (Part 1) 1934.

– *Filosofskaja nauka v SSSR za 25 let.* 1943. (Excerpts in: *Twenty-Five Years of Philosophy in the USSR.* In: Philosophy 1944, 72).

– *V.I. Lenin – velikij materialist-dialektik.* Kommunist 1955, 7.

MÖBUS, G.: *Bolschewistische Parteilichkeit als Leitmotiv der sowjetzonalen Kulturpolitik.* 1952.

– *Behauptung ohne Beweis.* Osnabrück. 1961.

MOČALIN, D. N.: *Rasovye teorii na službe amerikanskogo imperializma.* VF 1948, 4.

MONNEROT, J.: *Sociologie du communisme.* Paris. 1949. (Germ. 1952; Engl. 1953).

MORA, S. and P. ZWIERNIAK: *Giustizia Sovietica.* 1945.

MÜLLER-CHRISTIAN, S.: *Die physikalischen Thesen des Diamat.* Ost-Probleme 1957.

MÜLLER-MARKUS, S.: *Physikalischer Materiebegriff und dialektischer Materialismus.* In: Osteuropa Naturwissenschaft 1958, 2, 114–122.

– *Der Prozeß Einstein.* In: Wort und Wahrheit, 1959, 12, 755–770.

– *Einstein und die Sowjetphilosophie I. Krisis einer Lehre.* (Sovietica). Dordrecht. 1960.

– *Das naturwissenschaftliche Weltbild der Sowjetunion.* In: *Rußland – gestern und heute.* Bonn. 1960. 67–90.

– *Zur Diskussion der Relativitätstheorie in der Sowjetwissenschaft.* In: Philosophia Naturalis 1961, 3, 327–348.

– *Die Organisation der sowjetischen Philosophie der Physik.* In: Studies in Soviet Thought II (1962), 49–63.

– *Zum Anschaulichkeitsproblem in der Quanten-mechanik.* In: Studies in Soviet Thought II (1962), 289–300.

– *Bibliography of Philosophical Articles in* Uspexi fizičeskix nauk. In: Studies in Soviet Thought II (1962) 255–260.

Naučnaja sessija posvjaščennaja problemom fiziologičeskogo učenija Akademika I. P. Pavlova. 1950.

O diskussijax v naučnyx žurnalax. Kommunist 1955, 7.

OGIERMAN, H.: *Materialistische Dialektik.* (Discussion-article) 1958.

OLGIN, C.: *Lenin's Philosophical Legacy. The reconstruction of Dialectical Materialism.* In: Bulletin. Inst. for the Study of the USSR 1959.

OSMAKOV, I. I.: *Vsesojuznoje soveščanije po logike.* VF 1948, 2.

O položenii v biologičeskoj nauke. Stenografičeskij otčet vsesojuznoj akademii sel'skoxozjajstvennyx nauk im. V. I. Lenina. 31 ijulja–7 avgusta. 1948.

Osnovy marksistskoj filosofii. 1958.

Osnovy marksizma-leninizma. 1959.

PATRI, A.: *La Scolastique Marxiste-Léniniste.* In: Le Contrat Social 1961, 5, 279–285.

PHILIPOV, A.: *The Concise Philosophical Dictionary. A critical review.* N.Y. (Res. Progr. on the USSR). s.d.

– *Logic and Dialectic in the Soviet Union.* 1952.

PIROZHKOVA, V.: *Problems of Historical Materialism.* In: Bulletin. Inst. for the Study of the USSR 1958.

– *Freedom and Determinism in Historical Materialism.* In: *ibid.* 1959.

POPOV, P. S.: *O kurse logiki M. I. Karinskogo.* Spravka. VF 1947, 2.

– *Protiv putanicy i vulgarizacii v voprosax logiki.* VF 1955, 3.

– *Socialističeskaja revoljucija i vospitanie novogo čeloveka.* In: *Zadači sovetskoj estetiki.* VF 1948, 1.

ROZENTAL', M. M.: *Marksistskij dialektičeskij metod.* 1947. (s. Sviderskij).

– *Socjalisticeskaja revolucija i vospitanie novogo čeloveka.* VF 1948, 1.

– *Dialektičeskij materializm.* BSE ed. 2. 1953.

ROZENTAL', M. – P. JUDIN,: *Kratkij filosofskij slovar'.* 1939. (ed. 2:1940, ed. 3: 1951, ed. 4: 1954, ed. 5: 1963).

RUSSELL, B.: *The Practice and Theory of Bolshevism.* 1920. ed. 2: 1949.

SCHLESINGER, R. A. J.: *Prof. Kedrov on Philosophy and National Self-Assertion.* Soviet Studies 1949.

– *Some Materials on the Recent Attacks against Cosmopolitanism.* Soviet Studies 1949.

SIMON, BR. (ed.): *Psychology in the Soviet Union.* 1957.

Soveščanie dejatelej sovetskoj muzyky v CK VKP(b). 1948.

STALIN, I.: *Sočinenija.* 1946ff. (13 vols.).

– *Über dialektischen und historischen Materialismus.* Zürich 1945.

– s. Geschichte.

– *Lenine.* Paris 1946.

– *Marksizm i voprosy jazykoznanija.* 1950.

STRUVE, G.: *Histoire de la littérature soviétique*. 1946. (transl. B. Metzel).

SVIDERSKIJ, V. L.: *O knigax M. Leonova i M. Rozentalja*. VF 1947, 2.

ŠARIJA, P. A.: *O nekotoryx voprosax kommunističeskoj moraly*. 1951.

ŠIŠKIN, A. F.: *Osnovy kommunističeskoj moraly*. 1955.

ŠOROXOVA, E. V.: *V Institute filosofii AN SSSR*. In: *VF* 1956, 5, 220–222.

ŠOSTIN, N. A.: *D. I. Mendeleev i problemy izmerenija*. 1947. (s. review by K. V. in VF 1948, 4, 329ff.)

ŠTEJNMAN, R. JA.: *O reakcionnoj roli idealizma v fizike*. VF 1948, 3.

TAVANEC, P. V.: *Protiv idealističeskogo istolkovanija prirody suždenija*. VF 1948, 3.

TAVANEC, P., V. BOGUSLAVSKIJ,: *O prepodavanii logiki v srednej škole*. VF 1955, 1.

TOMASZEWSKI, T.: *O psychologii w ZSRR*. Kwartalnik Psychologiczny, Poznan 1947.

TROFIMOV, P. S.: *Obsuždenie knig M. Leonova i M. Rozentalja o marksistskom dialektičeskom metode*. VF 1948, 1.

VAGOVIČ, S.: *Etica comunista*. Roma. 1959.

VASIL'EV, N. P.: *O xode rabota Instituta*. VF 1948, 4.

VAVILOV, S. I.: *Twenty-Eight Years of Soviet Science*. Synthese 1946.

– *Tridcat' let sovetskoj nauki*. In: O sovetskoj soc. kulture i sep. 1947. (engl. Soviet Press Translations 1948, 2).

VOJŠVILLO, E. K.: *O knige 'Logika' prof. V. F. Asmusa*. VF 1947, 2.

VOLFSON, M. B., G. M. GAK,: *Očerki istoričeskogo materializma*. 1931.

VRIES, J. DE: *Die Erkenntnistheorie des dialektischen Materialismus*. 1958.

VYŠINSKIJ, P. E.: *Protiv formalizma i apolitičnosti v prepodavanii logiki*. VF 1948, 3.

WALTER, E. J.: *Der Begriff der Dialektik im Marxismus*. Dialectica 1947 (1).

WEISS, VON: *Logischer Positivismus und Kybernetik im Blickfeld der bolschewistischen Kritik*. In: Freiburger Zeitschrift für Phil. u. Theo. 1955. (Extract in: Ost-Probleme 1956).

– *Fundamente und Wirksamkeit der 'bolschewistischen Ideologie'*. Osteuropa 1958.

WERTH, A.: *A Musical Uproar in Moscow*. 1949.

WETTER, G. A.: *Il materialismo dialettico sovietico*. 1948.

– *Der dialektische Materialismus. Seine Geschichte und sein System in der Sowjetunion*. 1952 (ed. 3:1956).

– *Dialectical Materialism*. 1958.

– *Philosophie und Naturwissenschaft in der Sowjetunion*. 1958.

– *Der dialektische Materialismus und das Problem der Entstehung des Lebens. Zur Theorie von A. I. Oparin*. 1958.

– *Die sowjetische Konzeption der Koexistenz.* (Schriftenreihe der Bundeszentrale für Heimatdienst. H. 42). 1959. Also in: Aus Politik und Zeitgeschichte. 1959. – *Sowjetideologie heute I.* Frankfurt a.M. 1962.

WITT-HANSEN, J.: *Historical Materialism. The Method, the Theories, Exposition and Critique.* Book One: *The Method.* Copenhagen. 1960.

ZABUSKI, ST.: *Cyfry z za železnej kurtyny.* Intermarium (Roma) 1949 (4).

Zadači sovetskoj estetiki. VF 1948, 3.

ZELENOV, T.: *Izdanie i rasprostranenie proizvedenij I. V. Stalina.* Bolševik 1949 (23).

ŽDANOV, A. A.: *Vystuplenie tov. Ždanova.* In: *Diskussija po knige...* (VF 1947, 1). (engl. *On the History of Philosophy.* In: Political Affairs (USA) 1948 (4)).

ŽDANOV, JU.: *Au Comité Central du Parti Communiste (Bolchévik) de l'URSS; Au Camarade Staline.* In: Europe 1948 (33/4). (Pravda 7 Aug. 1948). (engl. Soviet Studies 1949).

NAME-INDEX

Marx, Engels, Lenin and Stalin are cited through the whole book on almost every page. In the Index, only those pages are indicated which especially deal with them or their works